MASTERPIECE

MASTERPIECE

*The Emotional Journey to Creating
Anything Great...Anything*

Dean Stoecker

Co-Founder and Executive Chairman,
Alteryx, Inc.

gatekeeper press™
Columbus, Ohio

MASTERPIECE:
The Emotional Journey to Creating Anything Great...Anything

Published by Gatekeeper Press
2167 Stringtown Rd, Suite 109
Columbus, OH 43123-2989
www.GatekeeperPress.com

The editorial work for this book is entirely the product of the author. Gatekeeper Press did not participate in and is not responsible for any aspect of this element.

Library of Congress Control Number: 2021951199

ISBN (hardcover): 9781662923135
ISBN (paperback): 9781662923142
eISBN: 9781662923159

Dedication

This book is written for and dedicated to anyone who is struggling with one of life's emotional journeys. Never be afraid to begin your trek, always forge the courage to get through the difficult phases that are guaranteed to confront you, and never go through your journey alone.

To that end, I am blessed with having so many people to thank for helping me along my journey and bringing that story to you. To my wife Angie, thank you for keeping me humble. While my 23-year dance was difficult, you went through it with me going backwards and in heels. You are amazing.

To my son Reed and daughter Abby, thanks for understanding why I was away so often. Part of our role as parents is to teach the value of work. To all of my grandkids—while I hope you will always remember me, please never forget my parents, Bud and Lollie. They were the definition of unconditional love.

There are literally thousands of associates, customers, partners, and vendors who have enlightened, encouraged, and inspired me, even if our time together was fleeting. Unfortunately, I can only thank a few of those thousands: Amy Holland, Paul Evans, Alan Gibson, Maureen Wolfson, James Dwyer, Margie Horvath, Patrick Emmanuel, Rafal Olbert, Lonnie Yenny, Tim Maudlin, Scott Jones, Adam Riley, Paul Watts, James and Joanna McGarva, Tom Brown,

Erik Weihenmayer, Langley Eide, Damian Austin, Jim and
Susan Wikle, Mark Frisch, Linda Thompson, Cornelius
Kastner, Abboud Ghanem, Jai Das, Kevin Rubin, Chris Lal,
Jeff Horing, Ken Black, Tara McCoy, Nino Pozgaj,
Octavia Harris, Jack Proehl, Keith Johnson, Rob Bryan,
and Nicole Johnson.

And thanks to Caroline, the barista at Diedrich Coffee in
Orange, Cal., who let me take employee interview calls
in her shop before we established our first office.

Contents

Never forget that you are one of a kind. Never forget that if there weren't any need for you in all your uniqueness to be on this earth, you wouldn't be here in the first place. And never forget, no matter how overwhelming life's challenges and problems seem to be, that one person can make a difference in the world. In fact, it is always because of one person that all the changes that matter in the world come about. So be that one person.

—R. Buckminster Fuller

Look at What We Built Today

I stood on the podium of the New York Stock Exchange, feeling dwarfed by the building's 72-foot ceiling. Below me, the trading floor was packed with more than a hundred of my employees, folks who had been with me for a very long time, wearing light blue hats emblazoned with our company's name. Among the crowd were family, friends, floor traders, and customers from the New York City area. Behind me on the podium stood a dozen more key people on my team.

In a few moments I would ring the bell for the Initial Public Offering of Alteryx, the data analytics company I had founded in 1997, 20 long years before.

The days leading up to this event were exhausting. I had turned 60 the week before and had been on the road for nine days straight, in every city, in every time zone, at every hour. It was the required "IPO road show" that sent me gallivanting around the country on a private jet funded by Goldman Sachs, talking up the company to investors in a whirlwind tour, from Minneapolis to L.A., San Francisco to Boston, and all parts in between.

I had never thought about taking Alteryx public until all other alternatives had been exhausted. I didn't want my hard work to simply become an opportunity for other people to make money. An important milestone, for sure, but I would never give the bankers credit for any of that. Yet at some point you have to raise money to accelerate growth. Our choices were to stay private and run as capital efficient as possible, sell the company to a bigger player to get leverage and scale, or raise capital and awareness by going public.

By March 2017, the moment for that last choice had come.

The night before we had a family dinner at Fraunces Tavern, the famous pub in operation since 1762. In retrospect, maybe it was symbolic that my long journey of many twists and turns would be celebrated at the oldest pub located in the oldest building in Manhattan. It was a blast, a lot of laughs, and a chance to re-connect with my four siblings to talk about almost everything but work. As midnight approached, we walked up Broad Street to our hotel, passing the main entrance to the Exchange. There, bathed in bright lights, was a gigantic blue banner bearing our company name and our chosen ticker symbol AYX, signaling our impending IPO, just hours away.

Now, standing next to me on the podium, John Tuttle of the NYSE opened up the thick guestbook to a blank page.

"Dean, there aren't many people who get to do this," he said. "Please sign your name to memorialize this day."

I was joining a very exclusive club. At the time, roughly 4,000 companies had gone public and only 65 enterprise software companies were trading on the NYSE.

I leafed through the book, scanning the names of legendary software companies and CEOs—Larry Ellison of Oracle, Jack Dorsey of Twitter, Marc Benioff of Salesforce, and VMWare's Diane Green. I was now moments away from joining their club.

For perhaps the first time, our IPO not only felt real but seemed surreal. I was standing in the same place where giants of the technology fields had stood before me. They had gone through journeys that couldn't have been radically different from mine. They had passed successfully through their moments of doubt, even defeat, as I had passed through mine. Although the specifics of those journeys and their outcomes were magnificently different, they were also magnificently the same. And our journeys were not yet over.

I recalled going back to my high school 25 years after I graduated, to show my wife where I went to school. We walked through the hallways and into the cafeteria. On the wall were photos and names of the school's most celebrated athletes. When I saw my name up there, I thought, *Oh, that's kind of cool.*

Now I felt the same way, but on a much larger scale.

I signed my name in the guest book: *Dean Stoecker, CEO of Alteryx.*

Moments later Tuttle said, "You see that clock right there? It's going to count down. As soon as it hits zero, push that button."

My first thought was, *There's no bell? You've got to be kidding me!* For weeks I'd been practicing hitting one.

I pressed the button, the bell sounded, and the crowd below me went crazy, whooping and hollering. I bear-hugged my son Reed and high-fived my team on the podium. It had been not only my journey—it was *our* journey. We had just become the only pure play analytic software company to go public.

Ringing the bell (actually, pressing the buzzer) at our IPO.

But as the crowd cheered and applauded, the moment felt oddly anti-climactic. Not quite hollow, not quite disappointing, not exactly an emotional letdown, but certainly not what I had expected. My 20-year "overnight success" had been an emotional journey during which I had seen and experienced the highest peaks of enlightenment, the deepest troughs of disillusionment and despair, and everything in between. That complex journey was hidden from the boisterous crowd celebrating on the Exchange floor. It was invisible to the NYSE officials clapping at my side. It was concealed from even my closest associates. What was supposed to be a moment of great excitement, an event that most CEOs consider their crowning achievement, the pinnacle of their careers, even a final destination, was strangely empty.

After I rang the bell I did a TV commercial for the Exchange, and then waited patiently for my turn on CNBC's "Squawk Alley." Most people would probably be nervous as hell before going on national TV, but I wasn't. However, my appearance kept getting delayed by breaking news about Trump, who was trying to get some big bill signed.

It seemed almost fitting that my moment in the spotlight was maybe less important than the national interests.

Had I expected it to be the most important day of my life, reality on a much larger scale was destined to set me straight.

Flying home the next morning with my wife Angie, I reflected on what had happened the day before. It had come and gone so fast. I was still nagged by that unsatisfying feeling.

Both my parents had passed by then. That was the hard part, because they didn't get to be with me on that seminal day. My success was based on the skills and values they taught me.

I grew up in a very blue-collar, middle-class family. I don't think my father made more than $10,000 a year. Although that might've been a lot of money back in the sixties, it didn't seem like it. There were five of us kids, seven of us living in a 1,700-square-foot house with one shower for everyone. We weren't poor by any means and never lacked for anything, but we learned humility, to appreciate everything we had, and to respect my parents' hard work that made it all possible.

As the youngest, I watched my siblings work together, pray together, laugh together. Every night around the dinner table, there was the ritual of the seven of us preparing and sharing a meal, talking about work and sports and school, and then cleaning up together.

Gazing out the airplane's window, I recalled the conversation I'd overheard as a child, for months on end. From the back seat of the car, I'd listen to dad talking about how he hated his job, how his ambition was to start his own business. Trained as a mechanical engineer, he built liquid nitrogen tanks for NASA, a mandatory product to make spacecraft safer. But at heart he was a right-brained thinker—a tinkerer, an experimenter, a creative risk-taker, an entrepreneur—stuck in a left-brained job, an analytically-oriented and precision-based occupation based on what others dictated. It wasn't very fulfilling, and I could hear the resignation permeate his conversations with mom as I listened from the back seat.

"Crymenetly," he muttered, a made-up word he used whenever he was unhappy about something. "I'm bored to tears. I don't know how much longer I can keep doing it."

"It's not that bad, Bud," mom said, "is it?"

"I hate the job, Lol. I want to start my own business."

"But there's a lot of risk in that. We have a mortgage, five kids."

"I can't do it anymore. I want to go out on my own."

"Okay, Bud, then go start your business. But let's make sure it's something the kids can work in, too, to teach them skills and help them save money for college."

Eventually he quit his job as mom cried. He took an established market and found a new and more efficient way of doing business. He founded Delta Vacation Homes—he would build A-frame houses in just a matter of days throughout the Colorado mountains, a quick and practical answer to a growing demand.

I was probably 12 years old when I started working for my dad on weekends, earning five bucks an hour to sweep up his shop. My brothers already worked in the business, each supervising construction crews of 4 or 5 people. There was an aura of intrigue about them being away for the summer and I wanted to do the same thing.

By watching my dad, I learned that there was nothing beneath me. If he asked me to pack up boxes, I did it. If he asked me to water the plants and the trees in the showroom, same thing. I took on those tasks without complaint because I had watched him do them. Working for my dad was a chance to understand how he managed his business, which was so cyclical, boom or bust. He'd have 50 or 60 employees working for him in the summer, but maybe one in the off-season.

By the time I was 18, I too had a construction crew of three teenagers working for me, building houses in five days all summer. I knew it was significant because it meant that my father trusted me, that he would never give me anything I couldn't handle, that I was ready to accept whatever responsibilities he sent my way. I never expected my father to coddle or take care of me. He challenged me to learn and to grow.

Everyone in my crew was within a year of my age, so I was their peer. I wasn't a crew boss who sat in a lawn chair on the job site, barking orders. I was a player/coach, a role I've played throughout my career. As a carpenter who loved to build things with my hands, I was right in there among them, hammering and sawing. I never asked them to do anything I wasn't willing to do. In the process, I learned that leadership is about making tough decisions, being industrious, and often improvising. When the weather's bad, do you keep working? What if someone becomes sick and you're 50 miles from the nearest clinic? What if someone gets injured?

Dad delivered truckloads of pre-cut lumber to the job site, so I knew that if anything became too difficult I could pick up the phone and call him. He would never put us in a position where we had to make tough decisions without his support.

I carried these lessons forward in my career—the importance of trusting my boss and my peers. When I became the boss, I wanted my colleagues to know that I was going to keep them out of danger wherever possible, while still pushing them to take on more responsibilities and to be better at what they did.

As a crew leader, I learned my strengths and weaknesses. There were guys on my crew who were stronger than me, so I literally had them do the heavy lifting. Other guys weren't very precise, so I didn't choose them for finish work. I learned how to leverage people's skillsets to the work that needed to be done.

My father gave us a per diem of $13 per person—$52 to cover breakfast, lunch, dinner, beer, snacks, and a motel room for a crew of four. We wanted to have fun after work, not be slaves to our job, so the four of us learned to economize. We'd cram into a motel room with two king-sized beds. We'd take the mattresses off the beds, and each of us would have either a mattress or a box spring to sleep on for the next five nights. (Every morning we put the beds back together to not inconvenience the cleaning crew.) This arrangement gave us beer money at the end of the day.

Because I was their peer, I felt what my coworkers felt. We worked grueling ten-hour days under the fierce Colorado sun, from eight in the morning to six at night, with a 30-minute break for lunch. My father's genius was designing a process that could build a pre-cut A-frame house in just five days, but that schedule inevitably took its toll.

At the end of one especially long day, we were heading back to the motel in the van, totally beat. When you get that exhausted you lose sight of the prize, the accomplishment. The satisfaction and joys of work are gone. It becomes just a job, a routine, an act of simply going through the motions. Not only is that not fun, it can lead to burnout, shoddy work, even accidents.

I had to do something to acknowledge what we were feeling, so I stopped the van alongside the road. Maybe we were a half-mile from the job site.

"Hey guys, get out for a minute."

They looked at each other, wondering what I was up to. The last thing they wanted to do right then was move their bodies.

"C'mon guys, it will take just a second."

Groans and moans, a few weary cusswords, but they roused themselves, climbed out, and stood with me alongside the road, their expressions baffled.

"What's up, Dean?"

"What's going on?"

I pointed in the distance at the outlines of the houses, the raw lumber a stark contrast against the dull green of the Colorado ponderosa pines.

"Gentlemen, look at what we built today," I called out. "Would you look at that masterpiece!"

We began high-fiving and chest-bumping one another, pumping our fists and whooping it up. The celebration over, we climbed back in the van and drove off down the road, raising a cloud of dust behind us. We weren't talking much more than before, but I could sense the energy in the van had shifted. We knew what we had accomplished, and we were tired now in a different way.

At the end of every day, when I leave the world headquarters of Alteryx Inc., a multi-billion-dollar company, I stop my car, gaze up at the building, envision our 1,500 employees, and say aloud: "Ladies and gentlemen, look at what we built today."

Creating anything of value in life almost always requires an emotional journey with many twists and turns—peaks of enlightenment, troughs of disillusionment, even moments of total capitulation. This is the inevitable part of creating anything great, and not just a great business.

I first heard of the emotional journey about five years ago, from a TED Talk. It's not something I invented, although I had clearly lived it, but until I listened to that talk I don't think I recognized the emotional journey I had been on all along. With its recognizable stages along the way, it was a construct that made me immediately say: *that's me.* And not just me, but almost everyone I've known or encountered, including great thinkers and innovators I've never met.

And it's you as well. All of us long to create something of lasting value—a great career, a fantastic marriage, a loving family or friendship, a stunning painting, a spellbinding book, or, if you're so inclined, an amazing business—a masterpiece in one form or another. But unless you can endure and navigate and learn from the emotional journey that your dream entails, unless you can rely on your family, friends, higher power, and a bit of humor to get you through, you'll never be able to ring the bell of success, however you define it.

I'm immensely proud of what we've accomplished at Alteryx. We've made data science easy through a simple drag-and-drop, click-and-run design. It lets anyone turn lifeless data into actionable insights possessing powerful outcomes. We have democratized the data science and machine learning world by putting the thrill back into problem solving in a low-code, no-code platform. When customers tell you they want to name their babies Alteryx, you know you're impacting people's lives.

Today our software is used in more than 90 countries and almost every industry. Coca-Cola uses Alteryx to help restaurants predict how much syrup to order, airlines to hedge the price of jet fuel, and banks to model derivatives.

And yes, we raised $144 million at the Alteryx IPO. But the next leg of the journey has just begun.

That's because success isn't an end point. It isn't even something that's material. In life you don't "accomplish something" and then stop. Success means that you become that person who wants to keep going, who takes another journey, and who faces the inevitable obstacles that will always crop up.

I get frustrated with entrepreneurs and CEOs, particularly those in Silicon Valley, who talk about "building unicorns"—the term used in the venture capital industry to describe a private company with a value over $1 billion. For many, that valuation becomes the sole focus of the journey. There's also the phrase "monster truck," a company with a $500 million valuation growing at a 50% annual clip. Or "burn rate," another favorite Silicon Valley term, meaning the pace at which a new company is spending its venture capital to finance overhead before generating positive cash flow from operations. I went without VC money for 14 years, choosing to focus on capital efficiency.

I don't think building anything great is about how much money you make, or how much you're worth, or what nest egg you've put together. And it's not about how quickly you accomplish what you set out to do. In my journey I was the tortoise, not the hare.

I'm not minimizing the benefits of having made a lot of money. I know many people would want to be in my shoes. I know how hard it is to struggle day-to-day in this country, and in most countries around the world. But material success means nothing if you don't feel good about your accomplishment. Material success doesn't matter if you've inspired other people to create something great—perhaps not great for you, but great for them. My greatest joy thus far in retirement is mentoring young entrepreneurs about their emotional journeys.

Everyone has their own idea of what success looks like. You have yours, I have mine. This book is about achieving success, however you define it. More specifically, it's about the ups and down, the triumphs as well as the inevitable failures along the way. At one point I was ready to sell my company, to give up, to ditch the project once and for all. And then I realized that the swamp we all must pass through was an essential part of the journey—not just unavoidable, but absolutely necessary for eventual success.

That's the journey I've been on all these years—not just once, but over and over again. It wasn't a journey of a single despondent valley followed by a single triumphant peak, but a constant journey of ups and downs, of mistakes made and repeated, of lessons learned, forgotten, and then re-learned. It was all those moments of thinking "now I've got it," only to be disappointed once again.

And I realized, in contrast to what most of us believe, that those ups and downs were what I most valued, most remembered, and would always most cherish. That was the experience I couldn't communicate, that was invisible to others, as I stood on the podium of the Exchange.

Yes, the Alteryx IPO was a significant ascent, but there would be no final peak. The journey would continue on forever.

This is not a business book per se. Sure, it will help entrepreneurs navigate the journey of building a business, but what I'm writing about has universal value that can be applied to any journey you might be on.

I don't think most journeys fail; rather, they get severed from the possibility of success. Most failures are not failures of vision or talent, but of belief and will. All too often this is because we choose the wrong passion to pursue, can't get through the dark swamp, or because we try to rush our journeys to get to some ill-defined or pre-conceived destination. I firmly believe that we have to be clear in defining success in any journey and be patient in seeing it through.

Starting a business is a daunting task—giving up a secure job, mortgaging your home to fund the business, never seeing your family. You must have courage to take this kind of gamble because when things get tough you can't acquiesce to your circumstances, throw up your hands, and say, "Well, maybe it wasn't such a good idea." It's too late then to turn back.

This applies as well to starting a family, making a marriage work, writing a novel, or maintaining a friendship.

No one hands you your future, but the people and situations you encounter on your journey can help you understand how to define and *own* your future. By owning, I mean sticking to your plan or vision, no matter what comes your way. I had many entrepreneurial failures before Alteryx and learned from each and every one. I learned what to do and what not to do through trial and error. I took calculated risks and more than once I failed miserably. Yet I kept taking those risks. I gave myself the ultimatum to either buy a business or start one. It was a huge gamble, and many times along the way I felt I had bitten off more than I could chew, that it was time to give up, to toss in the towel.

Every journey that we take in life will encounter that dark swamp of despair. The dark night can never be avoided, so therefore you must develop the skills and the will and the grit to see your way through it and come out the other end. I wrote this book to help you on that journey to your masterpiece.

The best part of the IPO, other than signing the guestbook, was the party we had that night at the top of the Freedom Tower, just a few blocks from the NYSE. I thanked our associates for all their hard work, my board of directors for their confidence in me and our mission, and expressed gratitude to our customers for putting their trust in our company.

The long day was winding to a close when a gentleman came up to me. I looked at his badge. His name was Mark and he was with the firm S&P Global, a customer of ours based in the city.

My first thought was, *Oh no, he's a data scientist. This is going to be a weird conversation. He'll get into the deep dive, algorithmic speak.* Which I wasn't in the mood for right then. I tried to front-run the conversation by simply asking him, "What's been your experience with Alteryx?"

Mark said, "You changed my life."

I felt almost a tectonic shift within me. When I talked to the media or gave press interviews, I always had to be on guard. But not now. I was fighting back tears.

"You improved not only my work life," he went on, "but you gave me back my home life and my family life. I used to get home from work seven, eight o'clock at night. And my wife, Lucy, used to come home at eight or nine. We had a nanny who helped us with the kids, but we didn't do homework with them or eat dinner together. It was a rushed life. We were using software that kept us slaves to our desks. And when my wife came home, she'd immediately go into her office and continue to work."

"Well, what happened?"

"I walked in one night and said, 'Lucy, I have to show you this software called Alteryx that I just downloaded.' She didn't want to be bothered and kept putting me off. I kept telling her how much it would help her. Finally, she agreed.

"I downloaded your software on her machine. In just 30 minutes, I showed her the incredible ways she could get her work done far more efficiently."

I said, "How is your life now?"

"I get home at 5 p.m. instead of eight. Now we spend a ton of time with our two kids. All of it thanks to your platform."

It was the most remarkable exchange I ever had with a customer. Tangible, real-life affirmation that my emotional journey had been more than worth it. Alteryx not only made his job easier, but we gave him back his life.

It was probably nine o'clock by then, the end of an extraordinarily long and emotional day, and that conversation was the beautiful nightcap.

In the days before the IPO, I probably met with 250 investors during my "road show." And yet today, looking back, I can't remember a single investor or much of what we talked about.

But I'll never forget Mark and the conversation we had that night. What he said meant far more to me than raising $144 million that day.

Chapter One

This is the Best Idea Ever

This is it, I said to myself. *This time it's really gonna work.*

"It" was my latest entrepreneurial venture, my latest brainstorm—the chimneyless fireplace. This one couldn't possibly be a loser.

It was 1985 and I was beginning to build a family. My wife and I had a young son and I was employed full-time at a data analytics company. Still, the ambition to have my own business—an innovative one—had never left me. On Friday nights and weekends I tinkered with ideas for my own company, much as my father had tinkered, experimented, and dreamed all his life.

One day I came across a firm that was selling chimneyless fireplaces. I was immediately captivated by the concept. Building houses for dad, I had experience installing fireplaces. It was not only a complicated job physically, but one that required meeting a lot of fire and building regulations.

The chimneyless fireplace offered a way around these obstacles. By simplifying the process for a product a lot of people found attractive, it had huge market potential.

It was a firebox that looked just like a fireplace, but it didn't require a flue because it burned fumeless grain alcohol. They came in brick and oak models, and were portable. Just a beautiful product, in both design and function.

I paid for the buildup of the business in California by selling them on the weekends, but I also did tons of statistical research, given my background in data and analytics. At the time, the largest apartment developer in the world was in southern California. My research compared the insurance costs of installing a real fireplace vs. the chimneyless version. If you were building a 1,000-unit apartment complex, the product not only saved an extra two man-days of construction per unit, but also saved you an extra $13 a month per unit for insurance, which meant millions of dollars saved for a reasonably-sized building. The chimneyless fireplace could mitigate massive costs for developers.

When I pitched the idea to the developer and his team, they loved it. They ran it by their engineering, legal, and insurance people. They also loved the idea of selling the fuel as a subscription service to apartment renters. If you're familiar with Software as a Service (SaaS), then this would be Fuel as a Service (FaaS). When tenants went by the rental office to pick up their mail, they'd also pick up another case of grain alcohol. I could sell the fireplace, enticing customers with the beautiful flame and amazing heat and comforting safety, and then turn it into a sustainable business.

The only problem was that I couldn't build the fireplaces myself. I had the skills but not the time. I had to order them from the manufacturer, American Hearthland.

I finally got my first big break when a chain of nine home improvement stores in southern California agreed to distribute the product. They anticipated big demand from apartment dwellers and office buildings. Everyone wanted a fireplace without all the usual hassles.

This is it, I said to myself.

It wasn't the first time.

My first stab at being an entrepreneur was sparked by a 1979 visit to a condo owned by my girlfriend's parents in Aspen, Colorado. I can remember Jean saying, "I wish I could rent this place without having to go through the association. They'll take 15% or 20% in management fees to rent it for me."

I thought, *She's got a pretty good idea.* Driving through Vail and Breckenridge, I knew there were thousands of condos in the area. I could pull the database of all the condos in Colorado, put up an 800 phone number, and we'd allow people to rent directly from condo owners, cutting out the associations.

I got as far as building the database, until I realized how much work it would take to market it, especially since this was well before the internet came to be. I had to abandon the idea even though it was a good one—the concept later became Airbnb.

New ideas were always coming to me. Since I had a full-time job I explored them largely at night, usually on weekends. I couldn't wait to get home on Friday to start fiddling with the ideas I had.

When attending a 1980 training program for my first post-university job in Ithaca, N.Y., I called the front desk and asked them to wake me up at seven a.m. because the program began at eight. There was no computer technology at the time to handle this task. The front desk forgot to call and I was late for my first training event. This happened more than once during the first few months of my career.

The thought came to me: *Why doesn't somebody invent a computerized system so we don't have to rely on fallible humans?* Living across from me at the time was a gentleman who had just retired from General Telephone Company in California, and we began prototyping a programmable phone that could call us at scheduled times.

This is ingenious, I thought. *We can sell it to every hotel operator in the world!*

Then reality hit—the cost of manufacturing the chips and other expenses. My partner estimated it would take at least $100,000 to get it going. As with the condo rental idea, I decided to pass. And as you know, every hotel today has computerized calling services!

I had good ideas, but didn't yet know how to execute on them.

They say that great entrepreneurs build a better mousetrap, but I don't think that's true. Great entrepreneurs are "disruptive innovators," a term introduced by economist Clayton Christensen in his 1997 book, *The*

Innovator's Dilemma. When you find new audiences for old practices, he believed, you can then build enormous value. Not a better mousetrap but an innovative one that disrupts the existing market.

Think back to 2010, when there were roughly 120 million single lens reflex cameras built in the U.S. Today the SLR has disappeared and all the camera makers are out of business, and yet we have 3 billion photographers in the world. Why? Because the mobile companies and the Apples of the world built cameras into phones that were better and certainly more convenient than SLR cameras, creating a new and huge audience for an old practice.

What's ironic about this is that the people who owned the patents on digital photography—Polaroid and Kodak—missed their huge chance because they couldn't disrupt themselves. They owned the technology, not Apple, but they couldn't figure out a way to reinvent who they were.

There are many examples of this. Blockbuster Video, for example, should have been Netflix. Sears Roebuck should have been Amazon. General Motors should have been Uber.

The digital revolution extends disruptive change far beyond the boardroom, permeating our social interactions, the cities we live in, and the economies we operate within. As the theoretical physicist Michio Kaku has said, the phones in our pockets now contain more computing power than all of NASA back in 1969, when we put two astronauts on the moon.

My father never thought that his job of building liquid nitrogen tanks was disruptive innovation. Frustrated and restless, he quit that job when I was still a young kid.

One day I saw him cutting sheets of wood in the backyard. What was he up to? Building a treehouse? Something for my siblings and me to play in? I was only four or five at the time, not knowing what to think. I just had the sense that whatever he was making had not been well-tested.

I watched the event unfold from our porch, side by side with mom, who would not let me out of her sight. She too knew it was an experiment.

There was palpable excitement as dad, my brother Steve, and my uncles assembled the structure, a Tinkertoy process of raising trusses in stages to construct an A-frame. I learned only much later that dad had been planning this new line of work—Delta Vacation Homes—for a long time. While he had sold architectural blueprints of the prototype in *Popular Science* for fifteen dollars, this was his first time actually building one.

It would be decades before I knew the term, but intuition told me that dad was engaged in disruption. He had reduced the process of building a house to a fraction of the standard time required, and he made them affordable to a much larger do-it-yourself (DIY) market. He was ahead of his time, rethinking old practices. Who wouldn't be excited about that?

Only a few hours had passed, and the frame of the structure looked nearly finished. "Look, mom," I cried out, "dad's almost done!"

At that moment, as they lifted up one last A-frame truss, I heard screams and shouts. Dad yelled, "Steve, look out!"

The entire structure was swaying. My 12-year-old brother jumped out of the way just in time, as dad's prototype tumbled down with a shattering crash.

I was 13 when I more fully understood dad's business, along with the depths of his hopes and dreams. He overcame those early hurdles, perfected his prototype, and bid on his first big job, building housing for oil field workers in Saudi Arabia. It seemed right up his alley—easy-to-build housing that could be put up in three or four days, roomy enough to accommodate large crews. And the Saudis wanted to buy thousands of these homes.

Once again, my intuition spoke to me—dad's business wasn't yet mature enough for that kind of job. At the time he had a seasonal outfit, building 50 or 60 houses in a three-month period. I remember thinking that even if he got the job, he wouldn't be able to pull it off. And sure enough, and thankfully, his bid was rejected.

Then he came up with another disruptive idea—motor home

rentals. He called it "Seasons Four" and spent a ton of time working on it. He was going to set up these RV rental centers around the country, kind of an Uber for motor homes. The customer would pay a fixed fee, and could drive a motor home from one Seasons Four location to another for vacations (consider it Motorhomes as a Service). But just as he was on the verge of going forward with it, oil prices went through the roof and the motor home market went to hell.

And so he hit his swamp again, but he didn't give up. He kept his focus on innovative ideas while balancing risk with reward.

It was his example of grit and determination that kept me on my journey. My next idea was Carrera, the portable crib.

In 1982 my wife and I had our son Reed. We wanted more kids, yet the thought of lugging around the necessary "stuff" for two or three toddlers was daunting, to put it mildly.

It was enough of an ordeal to visit our in-laws with just Reed. It took us two hours to pack the car—the stroller, the blankets, the toys, and the biggest, clumsiest item of all, the crib. By the time we got the car packed and arrived at the relatives for our "vacation," we were thoroughly exhausted.

After one particularly grueling trip, my thoughts turned to disrupting the crib market. How about a truly portable crib that folded up and doubled as a suitcase, providing ample storage for all the kids' stuff inside? After unpacking it, the suitcase would unfold into a bed, complete with legs and pop-up sides for safety. Three minutes after unloading the car, you'd be all set up and ready to enjoy your in-laws.

This one really excited me. I'd have a lock on an inexhaustible market.

Babies would always be in style and I'd never run out of customers. I'd enable millions of other parents to get their lives back. I had finally cracked the code.

That is, until I asked a manufacturer to bid on the large piece of injection-molded polyethylene that would form the frame for the suitcase/crib. The price tag: $250,000. *Ouch!*

Once again, I was naive enough to love the concept, and smart enough to recognize that I couldn't afford it. Once again, I never got beyond the idea stage.

Who knows—had I gone forward with the idea, maybe I would have had an army of kids!

And yet I didn't experience any of these ventures as crushing defeats. To me they were learning experiences. More specifically, I learned that manufacturing would be a critical piece of any successful venture. I had to fully understand manufacturing, and I knew I had to be well capitalized to pay for it.

Although I had no idea that I would someday build a multi-billion-dollar company, I was inching closer to Alteryx. I was learning more and more about what I could do, but more importantly, about what I was not equipped to do. I was gaining insight into how much I could rely on other people through outsourcing, and how much I had to do myself.

At this point I was already seven years into my career of selling data and analytics. I hadn't yet asked, let alone answered, a crucial question: *why was I trying to disrupt industries other than the one I knew best?*

You couldn't find a project more far afield from my profession of data and analytics than my next idea—Sensible Socks.

Everyone has a drawer of stray socks, those forlorn singles whose mates were left behind in the hotel room or mysteriously lost on the trip to the washing machine. Every Christmas I found it torturous to buy presents for my dad and father-in-law. They had everything—until I noticed one day that dad had a single stranded argyle sock in his drawer.

"What happened to the other one?" I asked him.

"No idea. I think I left it on vacation."

It was the era of the pet rock. *If they can sell that,* I thought, *I can surely sell socks.* An old and established market, craving disruption.

The sell came easily to me. *Do you buy your father-in-law another tie? Well, he hasn't worn the last four ties you've bought him. What about his stray socks?*

I designed a prototype of elegant cardboard packaging that looked like an expensive car, a Mercedes or a Porsche. Each package had a fancy rolled-up sock in the driver's and passenger's seats, and a third placed in the trunk, a replacement for the inevitable missing mate. This was it—Sensible Socks, a pair and a spare! A novel Father's Day or holiday gift for the man who has everything.

In contrast with the crib, my startup costs were low. I could buy the socks inexpensively, in thousand-lot orders. I could stamp out the cardboard cars pretty easily and inexpensively, much like the cardboard cut-outs for McDonald's Happy Meals.

This time it wasn't the money but the marketing that tripped me up. Was I really disrupting the sock industry? Was I enlarging the audience for an existing, everyday product? Or was I merely setting up shop in a very small niche of an oversaturated market? Do fads have long-term viability?

Answering these questions honestly, I abandoned the idea. I could always buy dad a new pair of argyles.

And yes, the success of the pet rock still pisses me off.

These were the entrepreneurial ventures under my belt when I came across the chimneyless fireplace. It was built by American Hearthland, a small outfit in St. Charles, Illinois, literally two guys. Like me, they were beginning their journey and didn't really have any idea of what they were doing. Yet I had enough construction experience with my father to see that their idea was ahead of its time.

In my data business "day job," everything I sold was subscription-based. That's what gave me the idea to apply that framework to a commercial product, selling not only the fireplace but the grain alcohol fuel, the first subscription service that I was aware of.

This was my incremental approach—stitching together various strategies that worked in other industries to see how they might come together in a new application.

I spent most of my weekends selling these fireplaces at local home improvement shows for $700 to $1,000 each. Perhaps I'd sell 10 or 15, but I knew there was the possibility of scale, even though the product raised people's eyebrows. How could you have a fireplace without a chimney? Would that be safe? Where would the fumes go? Overcoming that natural skepticism was the difficult part, but I finally mastered my presentation.

I knew that selling it through home improvement centers was probably a pretty good idea. I made the presentation one weekend and within two weeks I had orders from a home supply chain for 150 units. My first big break with a major retailer—I had a network, a chain of nine stores in southern California to sell the fireplaces. A very big deal. Even with 50-point margins in retail, it was a $100,000 order.

Obviously, I was very excited.

This is it, I thought, *this is the one.*

I said to myself: *"This is it!"*

I placed the order with American Hearthland and I was so anxious for it to arrive. I kept bugging them about the delivery date because the retailer was giving me a full-page ad in their weekly flyer on the day I was delivering the product to their stores, a couple of weeks before Thanksgiving and Black Friday. Perfect timing for the big sales rush.

I remember being face-to-face with the buyers, looking at the ad. I think they sensed my nervousness.

"Dean, we're going to run it in all of our circulars. You better not mess this up."

"Don't worry guys, I got this," I said, not sounding entirely confident.

The days dwindled down. Turkey Day was approaching fast. No fireplaces. I kept calling them and kept getting reassured.

The anxious retailer phoned me.

"Dean, what the heck is going on? Where are they? You better get them here pronto, because that full-page ad is going out to hundreds of thousands of people in just three days. The last thing I need is for customers to show up at the store and I'm empty-handed. The last thing you need, too."

As a customer-facing sales guy, I always rehearsed for both the likely and unlikely scenarios. Now I was rehearsing in front of the mirror or in the shower what I would tell the retailer if the fireplaces were a no-show. That discussion would be easy, but what I would tell my wife?

Finally, on a Tuesday afternoon, the day before the ad was to run, the shipment arrived.

Now I was really excited. I had weathered the storm and the seas ahead looked calm. I had figured this whole thing out. I was borrowing warehouse space at the time from my father-in-law. The truck rolled in and I opened up the back of the semi. I had tears of excitement in my eyes. I had ordered a combination of various designs and couldn't wait to see them.

I opened the first box. The fireplace was broken into pieces. My tears of joy turned into tears of rage.

They had six weeks to prepare my shipment, and this is what they sent?

I caught myself—maybe it was only the first box.

I opened the next one.

Another broken unit, a combination of crappy craftsmanship and poor packing. I built houses in five days with a crew of 19-year-olds. They couldn't make 150 identical units in six weeks? This wasn't rocket science, a product that required much complexity. They weren't ornate. They were case goods, like coffee tables or dressers. How could the quality be so bad?

I didn't say anything to the truck driver. What could I say? Take them back? If I did, what would I tell the store buyers who had been breathing down my neck for days on end?

So I focused on unloading the boxes. The truck driver had a forklift. With six boxes on each pallet, he made 25 trips into the warehouse. I signed for them in late afternoon and off he drove.

I was all alone in the warehouse and solitude is sometimes a great thing. No distractions. No one looking over my shoulder, saying, "Dean, I told you so." Plenty of time to reflect with the man upstairs on what to do next. I said the Serenity Prayer, about the wisdom and courage of knowing the difference between what I could and could not change. Then I asked myself, "What would dad do here?"

The answer came quickly. I had 150 boxes to check. And by morning I had to fix as many as I could.

Now I could cry without anyone watching me, not because of all the work I had to do, but because I had let my guard down.

Then I got hold of myself and my woodworking experience came into play. I ran out to a hardware store and bought a nail gun, wood glue, and stain that matched the fireplaces. I opened up every single box and went through them one by one. Not all of them were broken. Probably 20% of the shipment was damaged in some way, with a handful of fireplaces beyond salvaging.

For the rest of the night, I put in 20 or 30 minutes of work on each of the fireplaces that could be repaired. I didn't sleep a wink. Not only did I work all night, I then had to repack them in the morning, load all 150 boxes on another truck, and take them directly to the retailer's main store and warehouse so they could be displayed before opening.

I did all this myself and somehow got them there.

I was hoping they wouldn't notice the flaws, that perhaps I was being too critical. Maybe, just maybe, I had been too picky about the quality.

The next day I got a call. The retailer was quite disappointed. Because they arrived late, he didn't have enough time to merchandise them properly. They had planned on giving me great space in the store—the fireplaces displayed on staggered stair-steps at the entrance, so customers could really get a picture of what they would look like in an apartment, office, condo, or house. Now they couldn't do that.

They were mad and the conversation turned ugly. And I got it. I wasn't happy either, but I didn't voice my quality concerns to them because they had the right to return damaged items, which is common in retail. I didn't want to show my hand.

Three days passed and they only sold about half of the order. And there were a fair number of returns because of the damage.

I probably ate close to $250,000 when all was said and done. I had sunk a lot of money into it during the previous two years, developing marketing material for trade shows and creating promotional videos. When I tried to return the broken products, the manufacturer had gone bankrupt and I was stuck with them. Because they were in over their heads, I ended up being in over mine.

Each of my early startups had a swamp. Looking back, the closer and closer I got to realizing what my journey was eventually going to be, the deeper each swamp became.

The automated telephone wake-up calls and the portable cribs were easy ventures to abandon, as soon as I found out what they would cost. My disappointment was mild because I wasn't super ready to go ahead. There were too many things I still didn't know about starting a business. Walking away from them was an easy decision to make.

But the swamp I found myself in with the chimneyless fireplace was very deep and painful because I had put all my trust in the manufacturer.

I found out the hard way, in the depths of my despair, that the bedrock of every journey is built on trust. It's fundamental to every aspect of life. You have to be able to trust your spouse. You have to trust your kids. You have to trust your friends. You have to trust the manufacturer of your product. And you have to trust yourself, something I was now struggling with.

I realized that I couldn't outsource the most important parts of my journey to someone else. There were parts of my journey (as with anyone's journey) that were my responsibility alone.

I should have known better. I shouldn't have turned a blind eye. I shouldn't have cut corners or expected others to pick up the slack. Because I was good with my hands, I should have made the time to build the fireplaces myself. I had been building things for a long time, ever since I started working for dad. If I didn't have the time to build them, I shouldn't have been pursuing the project.

So this swamp really hurt, and not because I lost about a quarter of a million dollars. Money aside, I had spent tons of time away from my family at night and on weekends, and what did I have to show for it? Instead of the fireplaces being "this is it," I ended up suffering a crushing defeat, one that I had to own completely. What was unforeseen could have been foreseen, if I had only planned for it, anticipated it. I hadn't paid enough attention to the things that mattered most.

Yet what seemed to be my most humiliating moment contained the seeds of eventual success. It was a kick in the butt from somebody above: "Dean, don't you finally get it? You can't buy into someone else's journey. You have to build *your own*."

It clicked for me. *Build it yourself.* Just like dad did in our backyard, just like we did every summer for years and years. We built it ourselves.

All those Friday night experiments taught me that I couldn't succeed with someone else's idea. If someone else owns the intellectual property, you can't drive enough value for yourself. And even if you use someone else's idea, you can't let them build it. You have to build it yourself, to mitigate as much risk as possible. And this applies to much more than just business ventures.

If I was going to think big about creating my own business, I would have to own the creation and all its pieces. I couldn't rely on others to build the parts for me.

But after the fireplace disaster, I backed off from entrepreneurial experiments for a while. The next several years after that were a bit tough, as I took a break from the Friday night bug. I needed to give not only myself a break but my family as well. I couldn't put them through another torturous exercise in entrepreneurship. I didn't want to try to start another business until I found one that I was passionate about.

While I was disappointed in myself, I hadn't abandoned the pursuit of building a masterpiece. I knew there was going to be something else down the road. I recognized that dad and I had parallel journeys. His prototype came crashing down in the backyard, and my chimneyless fireplaces were a bust. We both had our respective swamps to endure and overcome.

Sometimes the apple does not fall far from the tree.

CHAPTER TWO

No One Loves Your Idea as Much as You Do

I went to work for a company in Newport Beach, Cal. called Integration Technologies, a small data analytics firm with a dozen employees. They had an interesting idea, but I saw them struggle with its implementation. The company was trying to build their own software, similar to what I had been proposing to Strategic Mapping, my previous employer. Unlike Strategic Mapping, which had fired me, Integration Technologies had an inkling of what I was proposing around technology and its value in the marketplace relative to geospatial analytics. Although what they were doing was directionally right, it wasn't what was needed to drive value for their customers and grow the company. I thought I could help them do that, and my entrepreneurial itch was suddenly reappearing.

The ideas I was proposing ultimately ended up as part of Alteryx's intellectual property—the notion that the ultimate value in content is when it becomes ubiquitous. The challenge is that achieving ubiquity is very difficult.

For most companies focused on data analytics, success is about doing three things exceedingly well:

1. Having access to relevant data that helps inform decisions.

2. Making that data accessible with easy-to-use software, so everyone can play with it.

3. Putting a complete layer of analytics around it that make the data dance, all to obtain better insights that drive bigger outcomes.

For companies that monetize data, the last two are critical if ubiquity is ever to be achieved.

I tried so hard to get my employers to understand these core concepts, only to result in "deer-in-the-headlights" looks when I brought them idea after idea that was summarily rejected. I couldn't get them to understand core principles in how to democratize data. Instead, they watered down their investments and became mediocre at everything.

The fundamental principle is that all data has a geographic dimension to it. A mailing list is not just names and addresses; they have latitude (X) and longitude (Y) coordinates for where each person lives and where every store is located. All the products in a store also have a geographic dimension, an XYZ coordinate corresponding to the location of aisles and the height of the shelves where products can be found. Everything that relates to any business happens in a physical location—where a crop is grown, where it's packaged, how it's shipped to stores, where it's eaten. And just as crucial are the people who live near that business and may become its customers.

I've been fascinated by geography since I was a kid, and my interest only grew during college when I travelled the world in a program called Semester at Sea. I've collected probably 50 globes over the years. Instead of taking lunch, I'll search out antique stores, finding glass globes, metal globes, globes that light up, baseball globes.

My career focus prior to starting Alteryx was all about leveraging geography to maximize business value because everything that happens in business happens somewhere. And if you could master geospatial analytics, I felt all other analytic processes would become easy.

Most people think about geography as being about the map, but in reality it's about the data. When you're using your car's navigation system, it's not the car that's helping you but the data that's guiding the car. And with autonomous vehicles, it's all about the sensors in the road and the digital street data telling you when to turn or to speed up or to slow down. It's not about the autonomous car or the map. It's really about intelligent data.

Geospatial analytics asks and answers fundamental questions. Here's an example I often use. Picking the location for a Walmart store is really hard. You have to buy or lease the land, build the building, inventory it, and hire a lot of people to run it. We're talking about a $100 million decision. If you pick a bad location and the store has to close, it has a huge and negative effect on all the adjacent locations, in addition to your brand being diminished. A crushing blow to the naïve business leader.

Enter data and analytics. Picking the right location isn't about having a good map to identify the right piece of land. It's about processing the complex set of data that surround that property, which is invisibly interconnected with that piece of land. It's about asking and answering fundamental questions.

- Where are current customers shopping?

- Which nearby stores are my competitors?

- What are their price points?

- How can I minimize cannibalization from my existing stores?

- How much is gas? Because if the price is high and the location is too distant, people won't drive to the store.

- How long is the traffic light in the left turn lane? If it's inconvenient to get there, if the drive isn't easy, people won't come.

All this data about shopping, competition, and traffic patterns comes into play and it gets very complex.

Geospatial data is a weird science, which is why most people don't get it. As soon as you say Geographic Information System (GIS) or geography, they think about a map. And for me, the map is the last mile of GIS. It's just a metaphor for the visual representation of a whole bunch of data.

Before Alteryx this was elusive to most people because geospatial analytic software was so hard to use. The data was not readily accessible and the analytics were next to impossible to achieve unless your Master's degree was in applied geography.

I'm a sales guy, not a software coder. I use software but don't write software. What I had was the vision for its application. What I was doing was revolutionary, and yet Strategic Mapping didn't quite get what I was proposing and pushed me out. The ultimate value in content is when you make it ubiquitous, and the only way you make it ubiquitous is to remove the friction between the human and the computer. This is the only way to get better insights that drive more meaningful outcomes for a greater number of users. These were the insights of J.C.R. Licklider when he penned his seminal paper *Man-Computer Symbiosis* in 1960. More on him later.

But Strategic Mapping didn't want to hear about analytics and data. They were all about the map and I couldn't get them to think differently. They just wanted to focus on mapping software, nothing more, nothing less. During a keynote address at the Business Geographics Conference in 1994, I said that "data is the rocket fuel for GIS, the elixir of life for a box of tools." But I just couldn't get them to understand that.

I kept pushing my ideas and they kept getting rejected. I was a loyal employee, as I had been in every job I ever had, but they decided to push me out because I was seen as a rabble-rouser, not a yes man. But I wouldn't resign. They had to fire me. Just a few short weeks after closing the largest deal in the company's history, largely driven by a focus on data, they did.

That's why I was hoping to be understood when I joined Integration Technologies in Newport Beach, Cal.

Because it was a small firm, maybe a dozen employees at the time, I thought I could have some influence on its product direction. They were doing around a million dollars in annual revenue by mostly selling other people's stuff. I learned from the chimneyless fireplaces that you have to make stuff yourself, and given my background I thought maybe I could help them build a better vision.

As their VP of business development, we doubled revenue in my first year. This was due to my salesmanship—my ability to articulate a story around leveraging data, analytics, and technology. I thought the founders saw the world the way I saw it—it's the data that creates the outcome.

Although I helped double their business, it was never going to be my business. They had three owners, a terrific husband and wife team of Glenn and Lisa, and an outside partner who in my opinion was obnoxious and arrogant. He would brag about his $400 Bruno Magli shoes, but he didn't really understand their business. He lived out of state, would show up three or four times a year, bark orders at everyone, and leave. His infrequent appearances were quite demoralizing.

The CEO was a really smart guy but not that willing to take risks, very conservative, which in some ways I liked. On the other hand, when you see opportunities right in front of you, risks that should be taken, you have to go for them. That wasn't their culture, their modus operandi. Because it was a family business, it was run like a family business—a place they could be sure to go to every day. Beyond that, there was no vision.

I was with the CEO in Barcelona doing a presentation at an international forum hosted by Experian, the large global data company. By that time we were still a small company with 17 or 18 employees. We were eating paella and sipping sangria together, and I said to him, "What do you want in this business?"

He said, "I just want to take care of my employees."

That's noble for sure, something I've always valued in my own role as a CEO and founder, but he had no bigger ambition. The best way to protect your employees is to build a more viable business, but he was comfortable with the status quo. I wanted them to press on faster and invest more to create more products and build the business, but on that we were starkly opposed.

After a year of working for them, I had come to a crossroads. I either had to start a business or I had to buy one.

On the 11-hour flight home I said to myself, *I have to make them an offer. I want a piece of this company so I can push them toward a more ambitious vision. After all, they were the first to really understand and appreciate my ideas.*

A couple of weeks after this trip I told my wife that I felt my career was a failed journey, that I was once again trusting too much in other people, and as a result I didn't feel I was "all in."

I didn't want to just collect a paycheck. I wanted to be more than an employee. I wanted a piece of the business to build something around my core vision—not around socks, cribs, or fireplaces, but something really close to my vision of data and analytics.

One morning in 1996, just days before Thanksgiving, I told my wife, "Today I'm either going to buy into the business, or I'm going to come back with a pink slip. I have no idea how these guys are going to react. Wish me luck."

I offered to buy the third partner's share for what I believed was far more than he deserved to receive, but perhaps far less than I was willing to pay. There was no negotiating, not even a discussion. They gave me an unequivocal no and fired me on the spot.

Looking back, I wasn't really surprised by the abrupt reaction. I had put them in a position where they couldn't win—they were either going to lose a close friend who was an investor or they would lose a strong contributor, and they chose the latter. Once again, this was an opportunity disguised as a setback. If I had stayed, I wouldn't have figured out my next move. Getting fired was the final impetus to committing to doing it on my own. Just like dad.

It was a warm day, and as I drove home I can remember rolling down my car windows and blasting The Who's "Won't Get Fooled Again" on the radio. I showed up at home, knocked on the door, and my wife opened it. She saw tears in my eyes.

"How did it go?"

I said, "Honey, we're in business."

She looked excited. "They accepted your offer!"

"No, they fired me. I'm going to start my own business."

Her excitement vanished.

"Well, Dean, you'd better get to work."

It was the greatest feeling on earth. It was more exciting than ringing the bell at the IPO. My tears were tears of exhilaration, not dread. The time was right, my ideas were good, and I would work as hard as I needed to bring them to life. I just wished that I hadn't waited until I was 40.

And yet I was also scared shitless.

I wasn't some young kid starting out. I had a big mortgage and two young kids at home. Scary for sure, but once again I thought right back to dad.

When he started his vacation home business, he had a partner named Joe. Joe wasn't an architect or a sales guy, but according to my father a mediocre operations person, and for several years dad was doing all the work. We used to hear him complain about how much he hated his NASA-related job. Now we heard him complaining about how much he loved his work but couldn't tolerate his partner.

It got to the point where dad reached his limit and decided to sell the company to Joe. My mom drove him up to Boulder and waited in the lawyers' parking lot for about two hours. She got a little antsy because she thought he was going to sign some papers to sell his portion of the business and come right back out.

Dad finally walked out and got in the car.

"I'm so glad you're done with this," she said. She knew how unhappy he was and she did not want to relive his previous work experience.

Dad looked at her and said, "I changed my mind and decided to buy his share out. So now we're the sole owners."

After her initial shock, mom was all in. She always supported him because she knew what his motivation was—not just to build an amazing company, but to build one where his kids could work alongside him, to learn, to grow, and earn enough money to pay their way through college.

Once again, I saw how my father and I had parallel journeys. He quit a job he hated and I was fired when my offer was rejected, and we both had to strike out on our own. It wasn't about the end point or the money for either of us. It wasn't about "success." It was about the excitement of having a vision and wanting to take the journey to make it come true.

When dad quit, he did it with five kids and on a much smaller income than I had when I got fired. He must have been scared shitless as much as I was, if not more so. I took inspiration from that—he survived, and I would too.

And that made getting a pink slip a very special day on my journey to creating something great.

When I told my family the news, they were a bit surprised. My parents and siblings didn't fully understand what I was doing. It became almost impossible to go to family events and holiday gatherings without encountering awkward questions, perplexed looks, and blank stares.

At one get-together at my parents' home in Denver, I overheard somebody asking my mom, "So what does Dean do?"

She replied, "Something with computers."

Either I was completely inept at describing what I was trying to accomplish, or they were too generationally challenged to understand the basics of what I did.

After all, my father's computer was a slide rule. While the slide rule got Americans to the moon in 1969, it was never going to solve the big data and analytic challenges of Walmart or give a harried worker his life back.

My siblings understood a bit more. And today, when they see the Green Bay Packers using Alteryx software to conduct on-field player analytics, they fully get it.

Now that I was on my own, I had to get some investment in my fledgling business. Back in 1996, if you had a pulse you could raise a ton of cash. It was the buildup to the dot-com bubble and venture capitalists were all over the place, dishing out ridiculous valuations for companies that had only a vision, no product, no revenue, no customers.

I called up Experian, the big global consumer credit company. I had worked for outfits that had partnered with them. Consumer credit is just a way to collect data that can be monetized for lots of business applications. Experian did that by building software and providing analytics, but in selling content to other people they were leaving a tremendous amount of money on the table by not leveraging technologies to make the data easier to produce, sell, ship, and use. They didn't have the technologies that would make it easier for customers to buy, year after year. They had the same challenges that all businesses face.

I thought for sure Experian would get what I did—the convergence of data, software, and analytics to drive value. How could one of the world's largest data companies *not* get that?

What I was trying to build was perfect for them. It was a no-brainer. I was addressing all the crucial problems they faced.

They spent an hour with me as I went through the presentation I had painstakingly put together and rehearsed. On the last page was my pitch: *I'm looking for half a million dollars for 25% of the company.*

They didn't express mild interest. They didn't say they would think about it. They didn't sound intrigued. It was, in their view, "a dumb idea." Right there, on the spot, they abruptly rejected my vision.

CHAPTER THREE

Thank God-fred

I was learning the hard way that no one's ever going to love your idea as much as you do, and you have to be prepared for that response in everything you choose in life. Some people won't like your idea because they wish they had thought of it themselves. Sometimes you're rejected because you're going against the flow of conventional wisdom. And sometimes your idea is too unique for people to fully grasp. But none of this has any bearing on the value of your ideas. The marketplace will finally catch up with you at the right time. Looking back, the challenge facing Alteryx was that we were way too far ahead in our thinking.

Did I experience doubt when my offer to Experian was rejected? A little bit. I wasn't thrown into a swamp by the rejection, but I started questioning myself as a messenger. I knew the message was solid, but maybe I still didn't know how to convey it. This time I thought I had knocked it out of the park in articulating the problem I was going to solve for them, but perhaps I had been mistaken.

The CEO's primary role is to make sure your money outlasts your ability to find the right product/market fit. You have to be a storyteller and persuade people not only to understand your ideas, but to fall in love with them. And that's hard. While I always believed in my ideas, it took me a long time to tell the story effectively.

The 25% equity I offered to Experian for $500,000 has been worth as much as $3 billion following our IPO. Not a bad ROI. But if they said yes and I took their money, I would've regretted it for sure. I never would have created the Alteryx that exists today.

Experian's rejection was the first sign that it was going to be a long journey. In fact, it took 14 more years for the market to get it, to understand the vision for self-service data science and analytics.

I still had faith that if I got closer to the users, like the real estate folks at Walmart who wanted to add dozens of stores annually, I'd be able to convince the market. How do you add those stores without screwing it up? How do you figure out the best locations? It's an extraordinarily hard problem. But if you have creative, curious problem solvers in the real estate department, they love these challenges. They love to figure things out. And I knew that eventually we could get these thinkers super excited about our platform, to solve really complex problems that no one ever thought could be solved.

The reminder here is that no one is going to love your idea as much as you do, so you must have faith that the world will eventually catch up.

And guess what? Today Experian is one of our largest customers. They spend way more than half a million dollars a year on our software, and, sure enough, we've helped transform their business. Some of their people have even said to me, "Where have you been all my life?"

And I say to myself, "Well, let me tell you a little story…"

Failing to convince Experian out of the gate, I went to my in-laws to borrow money because I was mortgaged up to my neck with the house. They also didn't like the idea or didn't fully understand it, and they were worried that I didn't have a full grasp of what I was doing. In almost every big risk or challenge you take on, people will question your sanity. My mother-in-law finally lent me the money—at a usury interest rate of 15%. I thought, "Where's the love here?"

After a few months, I took out a second mortgage to fund my fledgling business. By this point I was pretty loaded up on debt. Libby Adams and I had worked together at DMIS, SMI, and Integration Technologies, so she shared my vision for Alteryx. While she did invest some founder's capital in the early part of 1997, risk aversion was alive and well as I had to loan my partner Ned Harding $40,000 in order to bring him on as a co-founder. He was new to our circle so it was not unreasonable for him to be somewhat skeptical. So yes, I was somewhat financially stressed. It was an anxious time, yet that was a good thing because it forced me into action.

The good news was that I had gone through this before with the socks and chimneyless fireplaces. I knew I had to work my butt off. I rented a U-Haul and drove to pick up a bunch of office furniture being abandoned by a previous employer. Now that's capital efficiency! I used the loan from the in-laws to invest in equipment and hire another employee or two and pay them a reasonable salary.

My family was supportive. My father-in-law was also an entrepreneur who owned clothing stores. He knew the excitement of having your own business and running it. My in-laws may not have understood what I was doing, but they trusted me. They knew that I would pay them back no matter what. The loan was for a couple of years and I paid it off early. I didn't waste their money, which is what drives me crazy about Silicon Valley. A lot of entrepreneurs and founders go out and raise a bunch of money and then spend it on things that do not add value to the business.

You can either be a debt slave to others, or you can snap out of it and get your butt to the office and get stuff done. I understand the need to raise money, but I saw it as a weakness. VCs don't invest in you because of your good looks or good ideas. They only invest in you to get a return, and they'll never remember your name unless you pay them back. My father-in-law always told me, "Go get money when you don't need it because as soon as you need it, they're going to have you over a barrel."

So I always thought: *Okay, I'm going to build a business. I'm going to have real customers driving real revenue. Then I'll go ask for money because I'll have a better negotiating play than if the business is struggling and I'm begging for a line of credit at best, or venture capital at worst.*

But in the meantime I needed to depend on my mother-in-law.

While I waited for the market to catch up, it was the one-on-one encounters with potential customers that kept my head in the game. The innovators in the line of business, who were executing the strategies in the field, who understood on a visceral, not just theoretical level, what I was trying to do.

One was Godfred Otuteye, the CEO of a company in Southern California called Money Mailer. It was one of those outfits that sent saturation mail to households that included coupons for small businesses like barber shops, nail salons, and carpet cleaners. The company had set up several hundred franchisees around the country with their own territories.

Their challenge was to make their mail effective, efficient, and targeted. They had to make ad buys worthwhile for their advertisers. For some smaller retailers, a $300 ad buy would be their biggest advertising investment in a given year. Money Mailer had competitors who did direct mail, targeted mail, even though it was $20 per thousand households they were mailing to. Money Mailer had to make mass media attractive and responsive.

Godfred's head of strategy, Clarke Beauchamp, was a big idea guy. When we approached him he was open to us, but, like most people, a little confused about GIS. He thought it was all about the map, about where he was going to distribute his ad, rather than about using data to create a better media pitch for his franchisees.

Figuring out what advertisers they should sell to and how to pitch to them was a time-consuming process at Money Mailer. They had people producing maps for franchisees and that's all they did all day. They knew they had to automate the process through technology, so that franchisees could do their own work in identifying advertisers.

Godfred's goal was to democratize advertising research and that's where we came in. We were designing an application that would allow a franchisee to go in and identify what we called "Smart Zones." They could strategically choose what 10 phone calls to make to bring in advertisers to be in the coupon deck, and then how to automate their sales presentations to make the investment attractive. How many of these "Smart Zones" would an advertiser need to buy to optimize their media strategy? The advertiser could then decide whether to buy five zones or seven zones or ten zones from Money Mailer at $300 apiece, each delivering to thousands of households. The application that we proposed would enable them to do extremely targeted advertising to 16 million businesses, 100 million households, and 300 million people.

Godfred was from West Africa, a cool, sophisticated guy with a French accent. We had a couple of meetings with him, and he was interested. Our application was internet- and browser-based, which was unique at the time; today everything is cloud-based but not back then. Even though we hadn't built the product yet, we had put together the prototype of a structured query language (SQL) solution with bubblegum and bailing wire. I went against my best instincts and outsourced this development to a Canadian firm, telling myself, "You must make this yourself someday." A SQL engine is a relational database for performing calculations and database operations. Although the prototype was significantly slower that what we would later develop, it had tremendous amounts of capabilities.

It wasn't a question of wanting to get Godfred's business. We desperately had to get it. It was May 1997, six months after I got the pink slip from Integration Technologies. The cash drawer was running a little thin. So was my patience. We were trying to find that first dollar bill to put above the front door. We had given Godfred a $125,000 proposal for "Smart Zones." While he liked our resumes, he was a little leery about picking a no-name startup.

I relied on the discipline I had used for most of my career. I knew what was necessary to get that first customer. We did a couple of renditions of the proposal based upon feedback Money Mailer gave us. And I kind of knew that we were getting close, but hope isn't a strategy when it comes to sales.

I said to Libby, "We have to pull out all the stops to get this deal, and so we're going to try something that I normally wouldn't do, but I want to create some excitement. Let's do an open house."

I put together an invitation.

You are cordially invited to attend a special gathering of family, friends, clients, and partners to celebrate the formation of SRC—Spatial Re-Engineering Consultants.

I added an RSVP, to make it seem like an exclusive event.

It was all smoke and mirrors. We had a modest office, no product, no partners, three employees, and no customers. It was just me and my two co-founders, Libby and Ned. I was about to become a genius or a fool.

A book that has greatly influenced me, and that I will discuss at length in a later chapter of this book, is *The Art of War*, attributed to the ancient Chinese military strategist Sun Tzu and dating from roughly the 5th century B.C. One quote from the book became a cornerstone of my approach to any journey:

All warfare is based on deception. Hence, when we are able to attack, we must seem unable; when using our forces, we must appear inactive; when we are near, we must make the enemy believe we are far away; when far away, we must make him believe we are near.

I boil this down to an abbreviated phrasing: *When strong, appear weak; when weak, appear strong.*

To survive, we needed Godfred to believe we were quite strong. We went over the top to create the atmosphere and environment for that to happen. I put together a presentation deck with wireframes that looked like a live website, with Money Mailer's imagery and design, along with navigation buttons to drive the outcomes he would expect if he were to engage with us. Again, smoke and mirrors.

I hired a mariachi band and set up a Mexican buffet with an open bar. I invited architects from the firm next door to join us. We knew they would come for free booze and food. We invited our families. We invited some retailers on the street we had befriended during lunches. And we invited probably an additional 10 or 15 people—vendors and street sellers who we barely knew. They were just strangers for the most part, but we had to make the place look really busy and packed for Godfred.

When weak, appear strong.

I was holding my breath, but quite a crowd showed up. It started at four and went to midnight.

People were having a good time, eating, drinking, dancing to the music. I remember looking at my watch. It was probably 5:30, 5:45, and no sign of Godfred. If he was coming, it was going to be early. Had I had wasted 400 bucks on a Mexican buffet? And while the mariachi band was good, I probably wouldn't have paid them 250 bucks either. If Godfred didn't show, at least there was an open bar to drown my sorrows.

Just as I was about to give up, in he walks. He was wearing his signature smile and a polo shirt emblazoned with the Money Mailer logo.

The smoke-and-mirrors invitation that lured Godfred Otuteye.

"Hey, Dean, I only have a little time," he said. "I've got to get home to the family."

"Sure, I understand," I said. "Can I get you a drink?"

"I'll have scotch and soda." I brought him one and he downed it.

Then I gave him a tour of our office, all 950 square feet. It took about 90 seconds. You could see every corner by standing still. I felt I was showing him a Potemkin village, that he would soon discover the emperor needed to do some clothes shopping.

But I was super excited. Win or lose, I had accomplished the first task—getting him to show up.

He started asking about the business. He was a little nervous about being our first customer. What were our intentions? Were we going to raise money and if so when? What products we were going to build? Was this a business that had legs? What were our goals? What outcomes were we seeking?

I answered as best as I could. I didn't tell him this was an IPO with a Mexican theme. The only thing I was thinking about was getting his signature on that contract. I stuck to him like Velcro because I didn't want him finding out that the people jammed into our space and partying with the band were hot dog vendors and the antique dealers from downstairs. And I certainly didn't want him to meet my mother-in-law and find out about the 15% loan keeping us afloat.

After I gave him the nickel tour, I asked him if he wanted another drink.

"Sure, Dean."

I got him one, introduced him to Libby, and they talked about Money Mailer's need to not only sell more franchises but to help their existing franchisees become more productive to drive revenue growth. Although he didn't quite get spatial targeting, he knew it would be something very contemporary in an otherwise old-fashioned business.

Godfred finished his second drink and said, "Well, Dean, you have a great story and I loved hearing about it. But I only had about a half-hour to spare tonight and I need to head home."

He had had the last version of our contract for at least a week. Now was the moment to corner him into discussing it. I felt him and our company slipping right from my hands, so I almost grabbed him.

"Godfred, before you do that, can I show you something?"

When you're a sales guy, you always go for the close when the signs are there. But I didn't have all the signs yet because I needed to show him our storyboard of how we would modernize his business. I had spent the previous week building it to look like a real website.

He hesitated a moment.

"Godfred, before you go, please come on over to my desk. Can you sit down here and let me show you what we've built?"

Luckily my desk was three steps away. And so he sat down.

"Before we get started," I said, "can I get you one more drink?" Anything to get him to stay in place.

"Why not, I'll have one more."

I got him the scotch and soda. I sat down next to him and put my hand on his shoulder. He was sitting at table height, on a bar stool.

"Godfred, I think you're going to like what you see."

His eyes went right to my machine as I showed him "Smart Zones." I navigated through the screens and saw he was getting excited seeing how weeks of work could be done in minutes.

"This is what your franchisees will be able to do. And your team that sells franchises is going to be able to walk through three or four different use cases of how it can be done."

It was all wireframes. There was no database behind the scenes. There was no sophisticated integration of GIS or mapping capabilities. Everything was screenshots, with a click-through navigation that made it feel real. Even I was impressed.

I think Sun Tzu would have approved.

Like any good salesperson, I had rehearsed that demo about 50 times to make sure I covered all the salient points. After about 10 or 15 minutes I had pretty much exhausted all the screens.

Godfred said to me, "You realize that this would take one of our internal analysts a week to do? You just did it in 15 minutes."

"That's the intent," I said, "to make hard things simple."

"Dean, do you realize that you're going to revolutionize the ad media business?"

The words I was craving to hear. And not from an industry outsider. From someone on the front lines. From a potential paying customer.

Like any scared entrepreneur or good salesperson—take your pick—I pulled the pen from my pocket. I had the contract next to my machine, upside down, because I didn't want him to think I was laying on the hard sell. I turned it over and put it right in front of him, next to his now empty third scotch.

"Godfred, you're right. We *are* going to change the ad media world. And, as a start, I want to change your business first. Can I get you to sign this?" The $125,000 would be enough to pretty much carry us through the end of the year.

He looked at me and then the agreement. Did it again. And then a third time. I could tell he was a little tipsy.

"I can't, Dean. I think I've had too much to drink."

I stared at him, speechless. The peppy sounds of the mariachi band and the tumult of drunken revelry seemed to be mocking me. Good god, what had I done? It had all backfired.

Godfred stood up to go. Slowly. I kept my eyes on him, not knowing what to say.

After a couple of steps toward the door he turned to me. "But Dean, this is what I'll do. I will review the contract first thing in the morning and I should be able to get it back to you."

I don't know if I slept at all that night. I *should* be able to get it back to you, not I *will* get it back you. I kept thinking, *He's got to sign it, he's just gotta sign it. If he doesn't, it's going to be really hard to convince anybody.* I was worried that something else would come up in his world, that he would delay signing and eventually forget all about it. And as I tossed and turned all night, I kept second-guessing myself: *Why in hell did I get him that third scotch?*

The next morning at eight o'clock, the office fax machine came to life. There was the contract, with his signature on it. One of the most gratifying moments in my emotional journey. Someone finally had faith in our disruptive ideas and untested technology, and I knew that the next one was going to get easier, and then the next one, and the next one after that.

I called Ned, who had just signed on as our third co-founder, and gave him the good news. He asked me, "What do you want me to work on first?"

"Well, we've got to fix this SQL engine the Canadian firm built because the contract says Smart Zones gotta be done in June."

"Are you serious?" Ned said. "By next month?"

But Ned did develop it in 30 days. Truth is that Ned is a genius and I could not be more grateful for his technical skill. We both knew it was kind of a rush job, but we also knew it was the simpler precursor to the Allocate engine that we ended up building at the end of 1997 that would change people's lives. And today Allocate is still one of the more popular of the 270 tools in the Alteryx platform.

The next person who "got it" was John Bellizzi. He's now on our board and has been with me for 24 years.

In November 1997, he was head of business development for Thomson Newspapers, now part of Thomson Reuters, then one of the largest newspaper publishers in the country, owning over 50 daily newspapers, a multi-billion-dollar enterprise. They flew three executives out to California to visit with us. By that point I had five employees.

Thomson had the same challenges that Godfred had but on a grander scale—they were trying to sell ad space and do targeted messaging to customers. They wanted to build circulation by creating editorial content tailored to the demographic and psychographic profiles of their readers.

This is very hard stuff to do and they had hundreds and hundreds of salespeople around the U.S. and Canada trying to do it. Like Godfred, they wanted to automate sales presentations that were time-consuming to create, demanding a wide range of specialized skills. They wanted to enable their sales reps to create their own presentations.

We gave them an online demonstration of an updated version of "Smart Zones," showing them what we had built for Money Mailer. We had to leverage our first customer's belief in us to other prospects. They sat through the presentation and had almost the same reaction as Godfred.

"You're going to completely disrupt and transform the newspaper business."

They asked for a proposal and left. About 15 minutes later John Bellizzi came back up the stairs. I thought he had left behind a jacket or umbrella as it had been a chilly, rainy day.

He said, "We were sitting in the car thinking things over and we're so impressed. We think we want to invest. Would you be interested?"

Sixty days later we raised $1.8 million from them as seed money. I used a small portion of it buying desks for our new training center. I left the rest of it in the bank because I wasn't sure how hard it would be to find more Thomson Reuters and Money Mailers. Our ideas weren't crazy, but the journey was still young.

Celebrating angel investment with a round of golf.

Everybody hits a wall at some point, where you feel what you're producing isn't very good and that no one's going to buy into it. And so a large part of the journey—perhaps the hardest and most important part—is developing the ability to push through the inevitable doubts and roadblocks along the way.

You have to be persistent and persuasive. You have to care about and believe in your idea so much that customers will eventually come your way. When they do, it has a cumulative effect. When you see somebody turned on by your idea, it enables you to gain greater confidence to keep going. And a fellow named Andy Moncla was our next steppingstone.

It was May 1998 and I was manning a tabletop booth at a GIS software trade show at the Wharton School at the University of Pennsylvania. Andy walked by, introduced himself, and asked what we did. He told me he was a university-trained applied geographer who worked for one of the world's largest apparel manufacturers in South Carolina, VF Corporation, a multi-billion-dollar global company with lots of major brands, like Janssen, Wrangler, and Vans Shoes. As we talked, it was clear that Andy was quite knowledgeable in both MapInfo and ESRI, two of the leading software providers in GIS. Andy's job was to figure out how to get maximum sell-through for a product like Wrangler jeans at department, warehouse, and specialty stores, which requires a strong knowledge of how geospatial applications drive business outcomes.

My company was just twelve months old. We were still called Spatial Re-Engineering (we didn't become Alteryx until 2010). Our platform today has hundreds of tools with a wide range of unique capabilities, but at that time it wasn't really established. Our main tool was Allocate, which Integration Technologies had been trying to build and the tool I tried desperately to get Strategic Mapping to embrace. Allocate was also the workhorse for the Money Mailer and Thomson Reuters applications.

I gave Andy a description of what's called a block centroid retrieval system. It takes a look at the surface of the earth and calculates very quickly what we would refer to as "demand surfaces"—for example, how many people live within a 10-minute drive time (technically called an isochron) from a store.

Andy was immediately curious. The only way he could optimize the sale of men's 33-waist, 34-length Wrangler jeans in a warehouse store was to have a demand surface that quickly and accurately estimated the number of people within driving distance of that store who had that size leg and waist. To calculate this for thousands of stores using traditional GIS software could easily be a multi-month project.

I told him that Allocate could get him that information extraordinarily fast.

"It's especially built for the types of things you're trying to do."

"Okay," Andy said. "Why don't you type this in?" He gave me an address. "Let's see the results for a five-minute drive time around that address."

I typed in the address and the information came back in less than three seconds. Normally, it would take about three hours.

Andy looked befuddled.

"I don't believe that," he said. "When they ask me to do that for 5,000 stores, it takes me weeks. How was it done so fast?"

We talked a bit about in-memory computing and how the technology was not what he was accustomed to.

I told him, "We could do those 5,000 stores in about 20 minutes."

"Okay, well, let me just think about it." He walked away and browsed some of the other booths in the exhibit hall.

I could tell he was a naysayer, one of those guys who was deep in the discipline but who had doubts about something that was new, disruptive, and too good to be true.

About 15 minutes later he came back and gave me a harder assignment. "Can you do multiple addresses?"

"Yes sir."

The information came back in a few seconds.

"I don't believe this," Andy said.

He took another trip around the exhibit hall and returned with an even harder problem.

"If I gave you a list of a hundred stores I have on my computer, could you process that?"

"Sure thing, email me the list."

Done with ease and simplicity.

Once again, he was dumbfounded.

The next day at the exhibit, our dance continued. He came by my booth four or five times, each time with a more difficult question. Slowly but surely Andy was beginning to love my idea as much as I did.

"What about non-overlapping radii? If I have a bunch of stores within two or three miles of each other, I can't count those populations and drive times twice. I can only do them once, so how do you handle the overlaps?"

For retailers, accuracy requires making sure you're not counting populations multiple times. Eliminating overlap is critical to accuracy in merchandising, marketing, and store placement.

"Yeah, we can do that."

Andy's naysayer side came out. "That's probably going to be really slow."

I plugged in the information and it came back very quickly and with high accuracy, just marginally slower compared with other problems he gave me.

He kept upping the ante around complexity and volume. And each time Allocate met his challenge.

"I don't believe it. I really don't."

At the end of the two-day conference, I was closing the table and folding up my company banner when Andy stopped by.

"How much is this program?" I think we were selling it for $7,500 at the time.

"Well, when I get back I'm going to ask my boss, Pat Garvey, if I can get the budget for it. If I use your technology for all of the storefronts that sell Wrangler jeans—probably about 50,000 storefronts—it would save me countless weeks of work."

And, sure enough, about a week later, we got an order from him. We had turned him from a skeptic and doubter into a believer, even an advocate. Andy, who today runs his own consulting business, is an

Alteryx ACE (Alteryx Certified Expert), a very exclusive club with less than 50 people in the world who have achieved this "black belt" status. At trade shows he's talking up Alteryx to skeptics, just as I talked it up to him.

When Andy became a believer, it was a significant step forward. His purchase wasn't monetarily significant at the time, but what was significant was that he was the first person deeply versed in GIS to believe in and buy our platform. I knew if he got it—one of the really smart guys in the geospatial world—we'd overcome the roadblocks and the market would eventually catch up with us.

But if a guy like Andy hadn't gotten it, the journey of Alteryx would have been considerably longer.

CHAPTER FOUR

The Dark Swamp of Despair

The dark swamp of despair is never a single event. It isn't one cycle or one crisis you pass through on the emotional journey to creating anything great. Building a masterpiece is never that easy. In fact, while the peaks of enlightenment get higher, the troughs of disillusionment get deeper. Your disillusionment and despair increase with each setback because there's more at stake, the risks are greater, and you're more invested in your journey. If you fail, there's more you can lose, and not just financially. There are more people you can hurt, not only yourself.

I hit my deepest swamp in 2006. By then, nine years after its founding and the year we released our platform, Alteryx (still named SRC) had become a successful $12 million business. We were not only changing lives but winning over doubters. In fact, Experian, the company that wouldn't buy a partial stake in us, became our biggest customer in 2006.

So I knew we were having an impact, and I knew the vision was coming into focus. The evidence was all around me, to the point that multiple customers told me they thought of naming their babies Alteryx. A high compliment, something you never hear of in enterprise software.

Yet at the moment when I should have felt most satisfied and secure I was doubting myself, doubting my colleagues, doubting what we had achieved.

I had faced some rough pushback from competitors and companies who I thought were allies. My partners were resisting even the thought of raising money. I was disappointed that they didn't share my risk/reward attitude. I even began to worry that maybe they weren't in it for the long haul. When we leased offices Ned and Libby wouldn't sign with me, even though we were an LLC. I took the entire risk of signing expensive leases on my own dime. Simultaneously, I was going through what became an unfortunate and expensive divorce.

I knew there would be bumps in the road. I remember using that expression with my employees: "This is just a pothole we have to navigate around." But what happened in 2006 was much more than a pothole. It was more than a bump or a slight detour. It was the road off the edge of the cliff, to the very bottom of the swamp.

You get so blinded by the excitement of pursuing opportunities that you can't see the swamp coming. If I were to take my journey all over again, I would have the hindsight to be able to say, "Oh, I think I'm approaching a swamp." But I didn't have that perspective at the time. And so it was my deepest trough—the moment when I came to the brink of giving up and selling the business.

Why would I walk away from something I was so passionate about, that I believed in so deeply, that I had worked so hard to create over so many years, that I knew was changing people's lives? It seemed to go against everything I believed in and knew was possible.

That's what happens when you fall into the dark swamp of fucking despair.

Looking back, I've come to three conclusions about the inevitable swamp that we will all encounter, at one point or another, no matter what journey we're on or how much success we've achieved.

The first lesson is that you don't see the swamp coming until you're in it. It's almost like driving up to the Grand Canyon. The landscape is flat, not an obstacle in sight—until you reach the edge, and then it's a long way down from there. All the events leading up to my swamp were incremental. I didn't think they were leading me to the edge.

You're not saying to yourself, "Oh, I get it. Danger is approaching. I'd better be careful." Instead, after your crash to the bottom, you start reflecting. *How did I get here? Why didn't I see it coming? Why was I so blind?*

What seems obvious then wasn't so obvious before.

The second lesson I learned is that the closer you are to the people in your journey, the greater the risk of them becoming painful adversaries and unwitting victims.

As an entrepreneur you expect battles with your competitors; you even know that some competitors will fight unfairly and try to take advantage of you. I've been in court more than once because of that. But when your partners begin to do or say negative things, especially the ones you lent money to, it hurts a lot more.

And the third thing I've learned about the swamp is that most people are more invested in avoiding it than in facing it head on, coming out the other end, and ultimately finding success. You can't avoid the swamp, yet most people concentrate on mitigating risk because they don't want to get hurt any more than I wanted to get hurt. In fact, they often perform better in times of crises out of a sense of self-preservation and wanting to end their pain. But this attitude prevents them from achieving all they're capable of achieving.

In the early part of 2001, before 9/11, the internet started melting down. We had been growing pretty quickly and I hired probably 20 people too many. When the bubble was bursting, I told my partners that I'd made a mistake.

"We're going to have to let some people go because things are crashing all around us."

My partners jumped into action and we terminated the extra hires just like that. My partners were all-in when it came to reducing risk, and I appreciated them for that skill. But when it came to finding success in the business—raising money or taking chances on new ideas—they put up resistance. Everyone wants to mitigate failure, but very few people actually want to grab the bull by the horns and go all out for success.

There's a crucial difference between those two attitudes.

My two original partners, Ned and Libby, have been instrumental in the success of Alteryx. I am indebted to them for so much and I hope they know that, but I also had big battles with them through the years. Conflict is inevitable in every journey to creating anything great. Libby tended to side with Ned when we had conflicts, which drove me crazy.

Alteryx co-founders Dean Stoecker, Olivia Duane Adams, Ned Harding.

So I felt kind of outnumbered, even though at the time I owned 70% of the company. Based on our disagreements over simple things, I thought getting them to agree on the big things, like raising money or going public, would be next to impossible.

When I suggested hiring a bunch more salespeople to fuel the go-to-market side of the business, I got resistance. I remember saying to my partners, "Salespeople pay our salaries. Do you want them or not?" I overcame the resistance by giving each of them 1% more equity in the process. The resistance led to our Series A funding, taking nearly 10 months to complete.

They were afraid of the risk. Was I the only one who deeply believed in the eventual success the company would achieve?

Some sports teams have the reputation of choking in the big games, in the playoffs, World Series, or Super Bowl. Instead of playing to win, they play not to lose. You can never lose by keeping the other team scoreless, but that means you're not taking enough chances to put points on the board—to carry the ball into the end zone, put the puck in the net, or swish the ball through the hoop.

Whenever I interview a prospective hire, I always ask my favorite question: have you ever started a business? I'm not trying to find out whether they've failed or succeeded. That's irrelevant to me. I want to know if they've had the courage to try. I get super excited when I see success, but I never chastise anybody for having taken a chance that failed. Failure is the only the result of having had the courage to seek success. In fact, "result" is not the best word. Failure is the twin of success. They are inextricably bound together. You can't have success without failure. It's not possible.

Most failures are failures of will, not of talent. It's true that some goals are beyond the reach of our individual abilities. I was not born to be a concert pianist or an Olympic swimmer. Millions of young kids never became the next Mickey Mantle or Michael Jordan. But we often fail in areas where we do have talent and aptitude because we don't have the courage and the resilience to keep trying in the face of setbacks, and to take risks that can push us over the top and lead to breakthroughs we hadn't expected. In short, we often give up when victory is within our grasp. The emotional journey to creating anything great can wear you out and break you down.

I hired my current CFO about a year before our IPO. My previous CFO left the company because he was afraid of going public.

When I announced that we were going to do a pre-IPO audit in 2015, he panicked. And when I announced we were going for the IPO, he was gone. Why? I think he was afraid that he, not we, would fail and he wanted to mitigate his personal risk. It's hard to shake a "play not to lose" mindset. So he exercised all his options and got out. Others on my team left in the 90 days before the IPO and did not exercise their options, perhaps thinking we would fail in the IPO without them being on board.

I underestimated the toll that seeking success would take on me emotionally, intellectually, even physically. When these professional stresses combined with crises in my personal life, the difficulties became overwhelming.

Everyone thinks being head of your own company is a great idea, until you have to start making tough decisions that put you at personal risk. We had tried to make some acquisitions and we kept getting rejected. We were sued a few times, which I took as a badge of honor. It meant that we were successful enough to be a threat, that rivals were worried we would take away their customers. But lawsuits, even if you win, take their financial and emotional toll.

One company claimed they owned all of our technology because we built it for them on top of our intellectual property. I knew that we had hit a nerve, that we were impacting the market in a place that mattered, for a big organization to say they owned our technology.

But I had to file an antitrust suit to get them off our back and it cost us a million dollars.

Taking an OEM approach, we licensed our technology to another firm, MapInfo. This was a great contract and their margins would get even better as their volumes increased. The good news and the bad news was our technology became the fastest growing product in their history.

I've always believed that ultimate value comes from building things yourself. Well, they also came to that conclusion. Instead of making 60% or 70% margins on our stuff, they wanted 100%. After knocking it out of the park with them for two years, they wanted to buy us.

They offered us $10 million, 50% cash, 50% stock. I didn't think it was a very good offer, but I wasn't interested in selling anyway. I remembered my experience in trying to buy into Integration

Technologies. I said to myself, "If I don't sell, they're probably going to try and get rid of us."

So we sued them for co-opting our software as they built their own, except even after they built their own they continued to ship ours. It became a messy battle, but again, it was one of those situations where a previously strong ally became an incredibly strong adversary. More financial and emotional stress.

It ended up being a two-year legal battle. My partners wanted me to end it long before we did, but that wasn't my outlook. They wanted to mitigate the risk. I wanted to maximize the opportunity. And in that sense I lost the court battle but won the war—over the two years of legal warfare, we won back every one of their customers. I considered the $1 million in legal fees to be a marketing spend. Kind of a ballsy move when you're only driving $3 million in revenue.

I partnered with a software company in Boulder called Acme Software and started reselling their product in 1999. We did really well with it and our customers loved it, especially how we added our IP to theirs to enhance the offering. But at some point the company owner canceled our agreement and claimed that we owed him several hundred thousand dollars in unpaid royalties. This was another attempt to eliminate us as a competitor. They filed suit, we countersued and won, and they had to pay our legal bills. Yet it was painful because I had really liked the head of the software company. We won the war but lost a friend in the process. Journeys are hard. This battle cost us one year in software development and going to market, but became the final impetus to build our own platform. In 2006, we did.

All of these conflicts and obstacles were disillusioning. I knew that business was a contact sport, but this was an underside I hadn't seen before.

Most entrepreneurs will encounter this underside. Most people, on any journey, will become disillusioned at some point—about their goals, their partner or spouse, the path they've chosen. When that happens, the instinct is to cave, to get out, to mitigate risk. We're so afraid of losing that we don't see the opportunity to seize success.

I wasn't afraid of losing, but I was exhausted by the battles we had to fight. I was paying an emotional toll without really knowing it. I was getting incrementally closer to the swamp.

Most of us don't know how we'll react to the unexpected. After having never been sued in my life, in a short period of time I was going up against some of the most formidable legal organizations in the corporate world. One opposing attorney said to me, "We have an army of lawyers on the 47th floor, and we will destroy you." I didn't dare tell him that I was represented by a B+ lawyer who worked solo.

Another attempt to appear strong when weak.

But I didn't feel strong. Everyone seemed against me, whether it was my partners, my lawyers, or my competitors. I had vendors who'd been pestering me for the last two or three years. There was the relentless day-to-day grind of running the business, making the hard decisions, hiring and firing people, and working 70 to 80 hours a week, a schedule I'd been keeping for years on end.

I was going through a divorce, one of the worst things you can ever go through. And in the midst of all this, my wife's father passed away.

I knew nothing at the time of the "emotional curve." I didn't know that you had to reach bottom before you could make another climb. I had lost sight of the big picture. Rather than take a lunch break, I walked five blocks to Holy Family Catholic Church to pray. In the past I had come back rejuvenated and ready to resume the fight, but not now.

I had reached the absolute bottom and there was no way out. It was October 2007, my divorce nearly complete. My instinct was to sell the company I loved, the masterpiece I had wanted to build since I was a kid watching my father build his.

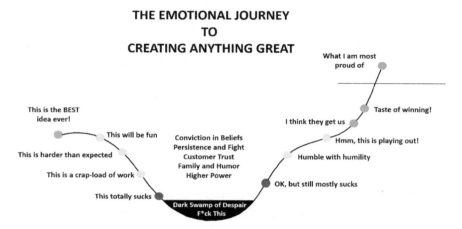

The arc of the emotional journey.

I turned to John Bellizzi, who had been head of business development for Thomson Reuters when we raised our seed money and who continues to be an Alteryx board member today. I enlisted him to assist me in choosing an investment banker to effectuate a sale. As a large shareholder, I needed John and his background to protect all of our interests.

I put together a full corporate presentation because our story wasn't well known, certainly not that well told, and I took responsibility for that. I didn't do a great job of spending marketing money in the early days, mainly because I didn't have the money to spare.

John sat through my presentations to each of the bankers, which took place in a big ballroom at what was then the Four Seasons Hotel in Newport Beach, Cal. One by one the bankers came in with their teams and I spent an hour with each, talking about our state of affairs and our opportunities. Each banker gave us their pitch on why they should be selected to represent us.

At the end of the long day, it was just John and me sitting in this big empty room. He could sense my anxiousness. My partners and I hadn't had much of an opportunity to debate a sale; they had no idea these meetings were taking place.

During our lunch break earlier, I had had a knock-down, drag-out phone fight with Ned about our users conference. He disagreed on almost everything I wanted to do. Here I was about to sell the company, and I was screaming at my partner in earshot of the investment banking teams.

How much deeper could the swamp get?

John broke the silence in the big meeting room.

"Dean, I've got to tell you, this is the first time since 1997, when you guys initially presented to us, that I've heard your updated story, and it's absolutely amazing, the best presentation I've heard. And I do mergers and acquisitions for one of the biggest information firms in the world. I'm going to go to the bathroom, and when I come back I want to spend a few minutes talking with you about your decision."

He got up and walked away. Being a CEO is a lonely job, but as John walked out the door I had never felt more isolated. When he came back, I knew he was going to make a recommendation on which banker to choose. My mind was made up—I was going to sell. It wasn't a 50/50 thing. I was literally at the end of my rope. I'd take John's advice on what firm should be my banker and I'd sell Alteryx.

He returned, sat down across from me, and said, "Dean, do you realize what you have? Let me run the math by you. And then you can make a more informed decision about whether you want to sell or keep going for a little bit longer."

For the next 20 minutes he put some figures together on a sheet of paper.

"If you sell now, you might get $30 million on an average day. If everything goes your way, you might get $45 million at most."

I needed that "most" in order to pay off my ex-wife and still have a meaningful outcome for myself. I wasn't up to my neck in the swamp. I was ten feet deep, in over my head.

"Dean, you're at $15 million in revenue. If you can get this thing to $25 million, improve your growth rates to 30%, 40%, or more, you can probably get a multiple on revenue of 6 or 7 times. The product has been out for less than two years and I think these metrics will be easy for you to hit."

Now, all of a sudden, here was the possibility of a $150 million company. With a paper napkin as a note pad, John put a value on my ability to get through the swamp.

It wasn't about the money. It was about the confidence he had in me.

When it's about the money, people are following the wrong thing. Our stock hit 140 bucks in August 2019. *Forbes* did a feature, calling me "the new billionaire." Two months later the stock took a big hit, down to $105 or something like that. They wrote another article: *Stoecker is No Longer a Billionaire.*

I chuckled over that because that had never been my goal. Yes, growing up I had joked with my brothers over who was going to be the first millionaire among us, but that wasn't what fueled my entrepreneurship. It was the creativity of building something that didn't exist before, the thirst to fill a need, to improve people's lives, to take the journey.

John used logic and math and analysis to get me out of my near-sightedness. We didn't talk about raising money. We didn't talk about selling Alteryx in the future. We didn't talk about the possibilities of an IPO. He basically instilled confidence in me that I knew what I was doing. That I was on the right path and needed to muster the courage to keep going.

He saved me from the edge of the precipice.

Winning deals with Godfred Otuteye and Andy Moncla were, in retrospect, relatively easy wins because they were sort of one-off deals. But this was the first time somebody said we had an incredible company, not just an incredible product. Sometimes you need an angel when you reach the bottom of the swamp, and John was that person.

And the funny thing is, it didn't take much for him to knock some sense into me. I'm a sucker for facts and John showed them to me. I had to overcome the fear of dealing with multiple problems. I had to come to terms with the emotional part of the journey. John showed me I could do so without losing everything I had worked so hard to build.

In the swamp, you lose your vision. You get so mired in something that you can't take a larger perspective. You're so blinded by what's been done to you (or what you think has been done to you) that you don't have the clarity to take action. And maybe I had taken myself and my problems way too seriously.

I called the bankers and told them I was going to keep going. John had saved me from making an $8 billion mistake. Now it was up to me to grab his lifeline, swim to shore, and climb up the rocks.

I turned, once again, to the lessons I learned growing up. I had to rely on my faith and my family, the values that mom and dad and my siblings taught me, through word and example.

I failed my first test as a college freshman, in a political science class. I'm sure lots of other people have done that, but for me it was the end of the world.

I was a great student in high school, took advanced placement classes, and got to thinking I was hot stuff. Maybe I went to too many parties. I wasn't hurt when I failed—I was utterly devastated. I couldn't bear calling my parents.

On a visit home I told them, "College isn't for me. I'm going to quit."

Turns out I didn't quit but kept going. I set up a meeting with the professor.

"I have to apologize," I told him, "because I know I'm better than that. I know how to study. I know how to prepare. And that wasn't me."

He was great. He looked at me and said, "First exam?"

I said, "Yeah."

"You know what? Bring your core competency back. And as long as you do well the rest of the year, I'll ignore that test."

So many failures are failures of will. Not a lack of talent or ideas, but a failure to be persistent in the face of adversity. The reason there's so much divorce is that couples find themselves in the swamp and say, "This isn't worth it. I'm gonna bail out."

When I hit my greatest swamp, the company was 10 years old. I remember thinking: if it was 10 years to the bottom of the swamp, it could very well take another 10 years to get out. As it turned out, the Alteryx IPO was celebrated 10 years later, almost to the day.

I once read an essay by the novelist John Gregory Dunne that has always stuck with me. In it he distinguished between the amateur writer and the professional. Both will repeatedly feel that what they're writing isn't very good, that it's nothing but crap, that they've lost their way, but the professional returns to the writing desk every day and continues on with the discipline of showing up; in contrast, the amateur gives up. The professional writer fights her or his way through the swamp while the amateur, up to the waist in muck, accepts defeat.

What is the oft-quoted number of hours required for mastery of any skill or craft? Ten thousand hours. And yet we're an instant gratification culture, where what we think we want is only a click away.

Andre Geim, the Dutch-British physicist and Nobel Prize winner, talks about there being only two kinds of people—travelers and tourists. If you're on a day trip, you're going to graze shallow. You'll look at interesting trinkets in souvenir shops and you'll enjoy a meal at the hotel. The traveler goes deep into the jungle of Fiji and sleeps in the King's hut (just as I did on my Semester at Sea adventure) because that's how he gets to truly understand what's most important about the culture. Anyone who starts on any journey needs to be a traveler. To go deep. Do not stay on the surface. Yes, sometimes it's good to be a tourist, to graze shallow for a while before you find your calling. Geim talked a lot about the importance of grazing shallow earlier in your career, before you've decided on your journey. You might want to date a lot of people before you commit to a marriage. Or you might want to take a lot of classes before you commit to a major. I grazed shallow in several startup ideas before starting Alteryx.

But you can't be a tourist if you want to survive the swamp. At some point you have to go deep. You can't skim and be successful. You're either all-in or you're out. You can't put a toe in the water; you've got to take the plunge. Whether it's your college career or your friendship or your marriage, you've got to be all-in. You've got to be persuasive in letting her know that you respect her and admire her and love being around her.

A lot of people give up in their journeys because they're not willing to do the hard work that it demands. They sever themselves from the possibility of success.

I said before that one aspect of the swamp is that you never see it coming. But I've come to the belief that there are specific stages that lead to the swamp and follow it, which can provide a framework for both anticipating its approach and recovering from it.

In 1992, before I started Alteryx, I was the VP of sales at a company that had merged with another outfit. I was tasked with making two divergent sales cultures work together. One was very outside sales-driven; the other was very inside sales-driven, a bit more aggressive and out on the edge. It was the biggest team I had led up to that point, and just after the merger I took them to a sales training/motivational event to help the cultures bond.

During the event one of the trainers made a statement that had a profound impact on me: "At any moment in life, there's only one of two states you can be in—you're either composing or you're decomposing. Those are your two choices, and you can't be in both at the same time."

Those are the stages on either side of the swamp. Understanding them may help you avoid the swamp or lessen its impact, as well as recover more quickly from its effects if it can't be avoided.

What do those terms mean?

A medical analogy best explains them. Say you have diabetes. Are you feeling good today or is your blood sugar low? Are you watching your diet and taking your medication, or are you eating everything in sight? In short, are you taking care of your illness or ignoring it?

You can't be in both states at the same time. You can't be doing healthy things and unhealthy things at the same time. You're either in one mode or the other. You're taking care of business or you're not. It's a choice, a conscious decision you make. The inability to know which state you're in can have a deleterious impact on your career—and your life.

The trainer was talking specifically about salespeople. A good salesperson has to be doing the tough stuff—searching down prospects, making cold calls, beating the bushes for business. You can't be a good salesperson with your feet up on the desk. You have to put yourself out there—proactively, energetically, with relentless drive. The business isn't going to come to you.

It's the same in any other endeavor. If you're progressing toward your objective, you're composing. You know tactically what you're supposed to be doing. You have KPIs (key performance indicators) that tell you whether or not you're on track. You know which state you're in, whether or not you want to admit it to yourself.

If I'm not very productive in my work, I'm decomposing. I can't tell you why I'm doing any of the work that I'm doing. I've lost the ability to get things done. I'm unfocused, I don't have drive, I'm wasting time and not working to my fullest potential.

When I'm composing, it doesn't mean that I'm seeing great results or outcomes every day. What it does mean is that in the face of challenges and doubts and bad days, I'm continuously working toward my goals. Composing is the sense that I'm growing in some way, that I'm learning something. Am I enriching myself? Am I taking positive steps towards solving a problem? Or am I avoiding a problem? Am I in stasis or taking action?

It's imperative that you figure out, every day, whether you're composing or decomposing. In fact, you can figure it out at almost any moment because composing and decomposing take place in each moment. Am I using this time productively? Is this thought or comment or conversation being framed in a positive way? Am I advancing or retreating, progressing or regressing? Am I taking care of business or in denial about what needs to be done? At this moment am I being as productive as I can? Maybe all I can do is something small, but the small things are crucial.

I've known both composing and decomposing very well.

Early in my career, when I was experimenting with all those startups, there were many times when I spent most of the day watching my office plants grow. But when you're out talking to customers and writing six proposals a week and closing a hundred thousand dollars' worth of business, it's easy to know what side of the coin you're on.

And this is not only true for salespeople and entrepreneurs. It's true for every situation, every journey in life. As a father, friend, spouse or business leader, it's your job to know when you're composing or decomposing.

In the case of relationships, composing means that you're not just enriching yourself but the people around you. This is what makes relationships so hard, yet so rewarding when done right.

If you don't have self-awareness about what's in front of you, dangerous things can happen. You can't get through your journey, especially the swamps, if you don't have that awareness.

I'm watching two entrepreneurs who are stuck in that place right now. They keep reinvesting more and more time and money on the wrong things that don't add value. They keep trying the same thing over and over, not realizing they're decomposing.

On the emotional journey, everything that's leading up to the swamp of despair is a decomposition of your faith, your hope, your trust in others, even your trust in yourself.

After you get through the swamp, albeit tough, you will emerge onto an upward slope that is a phase of composition—putting two and two together, realizing a little bit of success, having more empathy for the people you work with or the people you sell to or the vendors you buy from. When you're decomposing, you're losing control. When you're composing you're regaining it, and the original vision for your journey emerges with more clarity and purpose.

The key, again, is to have enough self-awareness to know, truthfully, without it being pointed out to you in a blatant way by someone else, what stage you're in. To know when you've met your match, to acknowledge that you don't have all the facts, and that you need help from others. To be willing to rely on family and friends to help you get back to composing. At every single bootcamp I ever led at Alteryx, I mention the old Kenny Rogers song—you have to know when to hold them and when to fold them.

On my drive home, I always ask myself: *What did I accomplish today?* If I can't name my accomplishments—and they don't have to be huge ones—I'm probably decomposing. And when that happens, I wake up, make my bed and start all over again.

After I decided to keep Alteryx, I navigated out of the swamp by keeping close not only the example of my father, but also to that of my brother Robin. He was a world-class gymnast who seemed destined for the Olympics. He was a straight-A student who could have gone to any school in the nation. Robin was composing.

He opted for a full scholarship to UC Berkeley, one of the top academic and gymnastics programs in the country.

Robin was a gymnastics supernova in high school.

The summer after his freshman year, he worked at a cheese factory in Denver to make some money. He hit a sledgehammer on a piece of equipment to dislodge something and a speck of metal flew into his retina; in a fraction of a second, his gymnastics career was over. He lost his scholarship and his Olympic dreams.

Robin wanted to be a neurosurgeon, but that's not a career you can do with one eye. It was a devastating setback, for him and the entire family. We weren't as athletic as Robin, but athletic enough to understand what a blow it was. Yet he figured out how to get through the dark swamp and alter his course. He figured out what he had to do to forge a new path. He pulled himself up from that setback.

He became a radiologist ultimately, had a very successful career, and ended up retiring early and well off. His mastery of the emotional journey resulted in a masterpiece.

There were lots of times when my brother John and I used to say that dad wasn't running his business right. We were on the same crew for a couple of years and we often had a larger vision for what Delta could be and what dad could accomplish. Being young, I think we saw opportunities that our father wasn't seizing. Youth also comes with a bit of ignorance and naivety, and we certainly didn't know all the challenges he faced. We did know that he respected us and listened to us.

Back in the early 1970s, he was trying to get through the worst economy Delta had ever experienced. The company had three employees—dad, me, and John, as our only other employee had gotten hurt and dad couldn't afford to replace him. He had gotten his business off the ground, but gas was now a fortune, interest rates were through the roof, and no one was spending money on either first or second homes.

In all the years I worked for my father, I only saw him get mad once, and it was during this time. One day at the shop, where he pre-cut the lumber before hauling it up to the mountains, he just lashed out at me. I don't even remember what his rage was about, only that it was so unlike him. I knew at that moment that the financial pressure had him at the end of his rope.

He had never raised outside money to support the business, but I'm sure glad he had a line of credit. He was a smart businessman and used to hedge lumber. He invested in futures so he could figure out how to price buildings 12 to 24 months down the road, but he didn't have a lot of margin for error.

I can remember sitting with John in a diner in the small town of Kremling, Colorado. We were now building big houses by ourselves out in the middle of freaking nowhere, just the two of us, because dad still couldn't afford to pay for more help. We were hoping and praying that he could figure out how to get through this hurdle, because the market was really tough.

John and I were sitting at the counter eating breakfast when the waiter said, "You guys want the morning paper?"

We said sure and he handed us a copy of *The Rocky Mountain News*. On the front page of the lifestyle section was a full-page photo of one of our A-frames, with dad standing on the deck. The accompanying article talked about how, with the economy showing signs of rebounding, people were going to buy Delta Vacation Homes. John and I had been telling dad for weeks to spend some time talking to the media to get free publicity. Apparently he had taken our advice.

My brother and I were screaming and hugging each other. The waiter must have thought we were nuts, but we were too elated to hold back.

With the help of family, friends, and his higher power, dad had finally gotten through his swamp

CHAPTER FIVE

The Tortoise and the Hare

The real estate market in Southern California in the late eighties was ridiculous, completely off the charts. There were dozens of new communities being built because the market was so strong, even though interest rates were relatively high. You could put down just $5,000 to buy a house. And you'd get that $5,000 back if you changed your mind because the builder knew he could sell it for more money.

And so I played around in the real estate market in Orange County, in both new and resale homes. It was a bit uncomfortable because I didn't really have control. No control over the quality of the construction. No control over whether a sewage plant was going to be built across the street. No control over whether rising interest rates would cause a housing market collapse before I had a chance to get out. Absolutely no control.

On the other hand, you could go in and buy a brand new house for five grand, wait the six months for it to be built, flip it on day one, and make serious money—50 or 60 grand a pop. You could buy resale homes, do nothing but throw on a coat of paint, wait 90 days, and sell for $25,000 more than you paid.

Yet I felt I was going against my core values, doing what banks do. They trade on what everyone else makes. They skim off other people's hard work. And that was kind of what I was doing, or at least it felt that way.

What's that old saying? When you fly too close to the sun, you get burned. Sure enough, the real estate market collapsed, I had a bunch of houses I couldn't get rid of, and I had to file for bankruptcy.

I learned once again that trading on what others have built is a lot less trustworthy than building something yourself. I also learned that if things happen too quickly, they're probably too good to be true.

In the software business, the tech sector that I'm in, you read every day about who's raising money, the strength of their balance sheet, and what their valuation is. Strangely, many first-time CEOs/founders seem to have pride in their "burn rate"—the pace at which new companies spend venture capital to finance overhead before they've generated any operational cash flow. Burning cash was never part of my vernacular.

When you don't have the money, you're kind of forced into making decisions that you wish you didn't have to make. I had to lay people off in 2001 when the tech bubble burst. After 9/11 we couldn't jump on a plane for months to see customers, the people who pay the bills.

The project with Godfred Otuteye, helped along by a little scotch, became very successful, but I couldn't replicate it fast enough. I couldn't hire developers or salespeople to do it again and again, to create the flywheel, because I didn't have the money.

That's the part that's hard. You want to go fast, but you can't. And so eventually the honeymoon ends, if only because a lot of decisions require capital resources needed for hiring talent, buying equipment, and investing in much-needed marketing. I can remember taking red-eye flights in the middle of the night, stuck in the very back of the plane because it was the only flight I could afford to get to a destination to sell our products.

And yet indebtedness doesn't get you anywhere. Silicon Valley entrepreneurs all too often see raising money as a badge of honor, as the final outcome, but to me raising money was a sign of weakness, at least until you perfected the product/market fit. It was hard enough for me to lose my own money; the thought of losing someone else's was untenable.

That's why I waited so long. I needed to know what I was going to spend it on, and I wasn't exactly sure. The product/market fit for Alteryx was elusive for a long while. It wasn't until 2010 that I felt ready to seek outside investment. The Thomson Reuters money in 1997 was just seed money. It turned out to be a phenomenal investment for them, but for me it was a safety net, a rainy-day reserve. I didn't spend any of it except fifty thousand outfitting a training center for both new employees and customers.

So 14 years after starting this journey, I began the process of raising venture money for the first time. I went to see a gentleman named Dave Roux of Silver Lake Partners. People said to me, "You have two hours with Dave Roux?"

I said, "Who is this guy?"

"He's the most successful and prolific investor on Sand Hill Road," a reference to the epicenter of venture capital for everything tech-related.

And so I sat down with him.

"You're looking for some money."

I said, "Yes I am, Dave."

"How long have you been doing this?"

"Fourteen years."

"What's the matter with you?" he said, his voice rising slightly. In other words, there must be something wrong with me, my leadership, or my business philosophy if this was my first time.

He didn't understand that we had built an $18 million business before I walked in his door. A business with real customers, real recurring revenue, no debt or burn rate. I don't think the VC world sees this kind of pattern very often.

"Well, Dave," I said, "I built the business the good old-fashioned way—slowly and carefully. I spent a decade growing the firm to $10 million in annual revenue. And as we waited, I kept the business lean, hiring slowly and forgoing outside investment, until I could build it up with meaningful customers and meaningful revenue. I wanted the market to open up before I went fast. Now at $18 million, while still reluctant to dilute, I need capital to access the $50 billion addressable market that is finally revealing itself."

If I had gone any faster, I told him, I would have burned a ton of cash and probably run out of money before I was able to find our market.

Silver Lake chose not to invest with us. The market was full of entrepreneurs with great ideas, large TAMs led by people desperate to get the VC funding badge of honor. I just was not one of them.

It may take a long time to trust yourself and to trust your views, and that's true in any creative endeavor. That's why it's often wiser to be the tortoise than the hare.

Every "overnight success" is based on years of hard work. There's really no such thing as instant gratification in creating anything worthwhile.

No one ever gets excited over a 5-year marriage. We get excited over the marriage that lasts 50 years or more. That's a journey. This is why the recommended one-year wedding anniversary gift is paper and the 50-year anniversary gift is gold.

Just as bad as giving up on your journey is trying to rush toward its eventual success.

Now, that can be an overgeneralization because there have been companies that have shot up overnight. WhatsApp sold to Facebook in 2014 for $16 billion and they had no revenue. There are people who fall in love on a first date and get married the following weekend. And I'm sure there are people who've been married for 50 years who fell in love the first time they saw each other and had a wedding two weeks later.

But those are the outliers—by far.

Building anything great takes time—lots of time. We can microwave food or we can cook something slowly and carefully. We know what's going to taste better, which choice will truly nourish both body and soul.

I watched my father build his business with care and patience. Perhaps I followed his example a little too closely. In fact, my blind spot might be that I've been too patient for most of my life, and yet I don't regret any of that because I want to give things a chance. I want to make sure that the decisions I make are correct. I don't procrastinate, but I am patient. We're all jaded by that amazing success story we hear or read about, and we falsely believe that's the expectation, the norm, the standard to judge ourselves by.

Joel Spolsky was the founder of a company called Fog Creek Software, and he had a famous line that circulated around the tech world: "Slow growth is slow death."

And I proved that isn't true. I suppose there are times when being the hare is wiser than being the tortoise, but more often than not the notion that going fast gets you there sooner is flat-out untrue.

Most of the people I was hiring in the early days didn't come from the software world. But after raising money and bringing in Silicon Valley people who were great at building, marketing, and selling software, I got crazy looks from some of them who thought I was not going fast enough, like they were giving me the Dave Roux eye.

I tried to instill in my teams that going fast is a choice, and sometimes it's the right choice depending where you are. When you see a market opportunity, you have to grab it. You may have to hire faster. Sometimes I've been the tortoise when I should have been the hare. Sometimes patience is a virtue; other times it's an albatross.

But there were more times when I moved too fast, and I've learned from that.

The key is knowing when to be the tortoise and when to be the hare. There were so many times when I would have loved to have gone faster, hired more people, invested in more marketing, and built our international offices with greater speed. I didn't build our first international office, in London, until 2014.

Our investors often wanted me to go faster. But when I saw the opportunity to build overseas and proposed the London office to my board of directors, they wanted me to slow down. They felt there was risk in expansion that I didn't see. I proceeded with London and it became a huge success.

The point is, you're never one animal. You're never just the tortoise or just the hare. You have to know the strengths and weaknesses of each, and how to be comfortable in each. You have to know the best choice for the particular situation you're in and adjust your techniques accordingly. And that only comes through the trial and error of experience.

In the early days I was certainly more of the tortoise. That's because the role of a CEO is to make sure the company survives long enough until you find the right product/market fit. Only then should you go fast, while still exercising caution.

A lot of people think that the higher you go or the bigger you get, the more control you have. Employees have often told me they want to be CEOs someday.

"Why?" I ask them.

"Because the CEO calls all the shots."

"Really?" I say. "I'm afraid you're sorely mistaken. You won't get to call all the shots, but I guarantee you'll receive all the blame if something goes wrong."

Business has so many variables operating simultaneously that it is very hard or impossible to predict or control what will happen next. There are no rules to guide you. You have to rely on your intuition and experience to make the best decision.

Any journey involves the unexpected, the unforeseen, the things you never saw coming and couldn't possibly have anticipated.

I heard a commercial the other day that said, based on today's social environment, you should have no less than six months of food on hand. I'm not the type of person who heeds that advice, who takes a survivalist point of view, but I do feel you have to imagine the unforeseen and prepare for it.

What happens if you don't have any money and get sued? What happens if your kid flunks out of college? What if he or she gets sick and doesn't have health insurance?

To build anything great, you've got to prepare for the things that you hope never happen, but that, unfortunately, are bound to happen in one form or another.

There have been times when I prepared for rainy days. When I raised the Thomson money, it gave me the comfort of knowing that I had at least six months of cash on hand. If things went haywire, I could still pay employees and vendors, even if I couldn't pay myself. (And yes, that happened on more than one occasion.)

At other times I've become overconfident. We were getting some traction back in 2000, even though our platform hadn't been built out yet. We had a couple of million dollars in the bank and I started hiring a bunch of people.

Then 9/11 hit and the dot-com bubble burst. I had been the hare without having enough empirical evidence to justify putting on racing shoes.

And I wasn't really prepared for a big lawsuit (actually two big lawsuits at the same time), one with another software company. We ended up becoming indentured servants to the lawyers—not the most pleasant experience!

But those are the things that you *have* to prepare for, even though you don't want to.

That's why it's crucial that you pick good relationships, whether it's your soon-to-be spouse, your business partner, or the friends you plan to lean on when the unexpected strikes.

I met my first wife Betsy in 1978 and we got married two and a half years later. That was being a bit of a hare. The journey ended after 27 years. Life on the road and a long, difficult journey take their toll on everyone, but I have no regrets. Betsy and I have two wonderful kids.

I met Angie, my second wife, in 2007 and we got married in 2011, a little over four years later. By comparison, I felt like a tortoise the second time around. She was instrumental in helping me exit the swamp gracefully.

Two journeys of the same kind; in each I was not the same animal.

I first learned the rhythms of the tortoise and the hare by watching my father.

Looking back, he had such an interesting business because for nine months of the year he was working all by himself, cutting wood all day long for houses that would not be constructed until the summer. For three quarters of the year, dad was a tortoise. At the end of May he became the hare. We had to build 25 homes in 90 days before we had to go back to school. A three-month building period and that was it.

The schedule was exacting and demanding. So, working with him, I saw how he paced himself to achieve his objectives.

When I did my Series A and A+ funding, raising the $12 million took me almost a year to complete, a snail's pace. Most Series A's happen a lot faster than that. Two years later, my Series B funding raised $60 million in five months at a $360 million valuation. Belizzi's napkin was spot on.

Series A funding is considered seed capital since it's designed to help new companies grow. Series B financing is the next stage of funding after the company has had time to generate revenue from sales. Investors have a chance to see how the management team has performed and whether the investment is worth it or not.

The Series C was done in three months with $85 million funded. We went public in a nine-day marketing blitz that yielded $114 million in fresh capital. Six months later I did a $100 million follow-on equity sale in three days. A year later a $230 million convertible note was sold in about six hours of telemarketing. And just 12 months later, we raised $1 billion in convertible notes in just 90 minutes with just a few phone calls.

Your journey gets faster when you have some experience under your belt. The hare of Alteryx finally put on running shoes.

It's easier to be a hare after you've gone through the trough of disillusionment. You're then better able to recognize green shoots of opportunity and your timing of events becomes nearly flawless. When people finally get you, it's easier to go faster.

Over time, you'll learn what speed to go.

CHAPTER SIX ————————

Trust Defines Integrity

A lot of companies say they put their customers first. They purport to have customer-centric behaviors even when they don't know what that entails. Too often, these terms become nothing more than buzzwords, a lot of BS and PR fodder.

Authentic and enduring customer-centricity is the only thing that matters, and I've boiled it down to giving the right answers to six questions:

- Is this the right product for the customer?

- Are we delivering the product we said we were going to deliver?

- Does it work in the way that we said it would work?

- Are we charging them the price that we said we would charge?

- Are we ensuring their success with the product?

- Are we listening to customer feedback and responding back to them?

These are the six questions that have to be asked and answered on a daily basis, with no shortcuts.

Most companies when they start out are inward-facing. Because they're trying to survive, they're more concerned about themselves than they are with partners and customers and prospects and people on the outside.

That's innately what we do when we take a big risk in life—we hunker down. When you put up a bunch of money for a mortgage on a house or take on huge student debt, you're scared to death. You're seeing those payments stretching out in front of you for years and you wonder if you've made a mistake. You're focused on what you have to do to make those payments and not lose the house or become a debt slave. You have tunnel vision that doesn't allow for other priorities. But as a business matures, it must become more outward-facing toward the customers it serves.

My background was in sales. I had to listen to customers, hear what they needed to say, and repeat it back to them for clarity. Part of our success as an organization was that I wasn't a technical leader. I wasn't the guy in the back office writing code. I was in the front lines of the company/customer interface.

Alteryx was always customer-friendly, but we weren't always doing the best possible job. There's a difference between being customer-friendly and being customer-centric. In reality, we had a lot to learn about both.

Our turn toward true customer-centric behavior began in the early 2000s when we approached Axiom, then one of the largest database companies in the world. They had big ambitions around delivering a cloud service, so people could buy names and addresses for prospecting, mailing, telemarketing, and things like that.

At the time we were still small, with only six or seven employees. Once again *The Art of War* came into play. As with Godfred I needed their business, they needed the solution, and I got very creative to make certain that happened.

As expected, they were very big on information security. They managed many of the largest databases for banks around the country. Their data center in Conway, Arkansas was ginormous—football fields long with thousands of servers processing billions of records a day.

They insisted on seeing our datacenter before signing, even though we didn't have one. Just like we didn't have customers or products or partners when Godfred showed up at the party several years before.

"I'll show you the data center," I said, "but first I want to meet you at the Boulderado Hotel and get the contract signed. Then I'll take you on a tour of the company."

My palms now sweaty, I got them to sign at the hotel and before the ink was dry they asked for the tour.

I thought, *How many times can I get away with this? This time I'm going to get nailed.*

I walked them up Mapleton Hill in Boulder. They were super excited. They were wearing suits, and we were in jeans and short-sleeve shirts.

As we walked I said, "Guys, our data center may not be all that you're imagining. We're a small company, but trust me, we know how to take care of data. We're great at making data smart, compressed, and secure."

"That's okay, we just want to see it. We have to check this off the list for IT governance."

We walked up three flights of rickety outdoor stairs to our 500-square-foot office, situated above a dental practice. Two employees were there that day, both wearing shorts and raggedy t-shirts, their bare feet up on their desks.

The expressions on the faces of the Axiom team were priceless. Thank god the ink on the contract was dry.

I walked them back to the kitchen. Our sole two computers sat atop a bread rack. "Welcome to our data center," I said sheepishly.

Next to the rack was our toaster. The moment the Axiom team walked in, two freshly toasted bagels popped out and were grabbed by a sockless employee. I was as stunned as they were.

"This is your data center?"

I forget what I said, but I must have pulled out all the stops. We passed all their security tests.

I also don't recall if we offered them any toasted bagels that day.

Now that the contract was done, they invited us to Conway, Arkansas, where we met them at a Holiday Inn on Toad Suck Square. Seriously. Maybe the address was karmic payback for the toaster fiasco.

Ned Harding and I spent two days with these guys and they had a very sophisticated effort—design engineers, UI engineers, graphic designers, security personnel. They had 25 people there for two days. They told us everything that they were looking for in the application that we were going to build for them.

For two days Ned and I took tons of notes. I was trying to be very customer-centric, listening carefully to everything, nodding when appropriate, refraining from shaking my head when I would have been justified in doing so.

At the end of the two days the leader of the Axiom team said, "Ned and Dean, I'm really happy that you guys came down here and spent the time with us. We saw that you've taken tons of notes. And we're so excited because we think you're really gonna deliver on exactly what we've talked about."

Before I could respond, Ned replied, "Well, we want to thank you too for being here and for hearing us out, but we're going to build it the way we want."

My jaw dropped. Two days of customer feedback negated in ten seconds.

After kicking Ned under the table, I covered up for him by repeating the major initiatives and timelines we had discussed. Then I yelled at him all the way back to the Little Rock airport.

"What is your problem? Don't you know how hard I worked to line up this deal? And you just about killed it!"

In the end, we made them almost precisely what they wanted, but only after we had almost blown the deal. It led ultimately to the development of Calgary, one of the most impressive tools in the Alteryx platform today.

Despite this near disaster, I had to experience two more major mishaps before I finally started our customer-centric program.

One was with Sprint, where they were using our tools and software in completely incorrect ways when I had assumed the right ways were pretty obvious. I was totally embarrassed—personally, and for the company as a whole. I had a meeting with the Sprint team and apologized: "We let you down because you're not using the software the way it was intended. We failed you."

Shortly after that I did a demo at Carl Karcher Enterprises, a big quick-service restaurant chain, and at the end of the presentation one of their people said, "Is this a cloud service?"

I thought it was patently clear that the parts I was showing him were not cloud-based, while those that were cloud-based were clearly running in a browser, but he didn't get it. And I took personal responsibility for that.

A couple of days later I attended a Gartner conference where one of the speakers was Don Peppers, probably the foremost international expert in one-to-one marketing. I sat there, exhausted from traveling, disappointed in my customer interactions. My ears perked up when I heard him say, "For all the entrepreneurs in the audience, just remember this—customer trust defines the integrity of your company."

That was a seminal moment for me. A moment that enlightened me into "alteryxing" the way our company would operate to this day. As soon as I got back to company headquarters, I called a meeting.

"From here on in, we're going to do things differently," I said. "I can't be embarrassed for myself, for you, or for this company, in the way I have been during the last few days."

From that point on, customer-centricity became a key measure for Alteryx. We track it every year with a Net Promoter Score (NPS) survey, and we follow every trouble ticket in tech support with Customer Satisfaction Scores (CSAT). We've improved on both in every year since. And we've built the number-one customer community in the world as measured by CMX, the world's largest group of community professionals. In 2021 we beat out the leading enterprise software companies in the world.

We've instilled in our associates that customers are the ones who pay the bills. I don't pay them; I just write the check. If you lose the customer's trust, then we're all toast.

Tech companies are often known for not providing good customer service. They take a long time to shift from inward thinking, primarily revolving around product development behavior, to outward thinking that focuses primarily on customer requirements. A lot of them misunderstand what customer-centric behavior is all about.

For example, a number of executives have said to me, "Well, we're not going to do everything that a customer wants us to do."

That entirely misses the point. The point is that you have to hear the customer and then respond to the customer, even if the answer is, "Sorry, I can't do that for you."

For many years, Sears Roebuck had a poster in all of their storerooms stating their customer-centric policy.

Rule #1 – The customer is always right.

Rule #2 – Reread rule #1.

But in truth the customer isn't always right. We have all witnessed the demise of Sears Roebuck over the last two decades. The customer has a view of what's right for him, but you have to balance it with running a business for all of your customers. Being a doormat serves no one well.

The key is being able to communicate back to the customer in a meaningful way about what can and can't be done, and why. The customer wants to be heard and respected; the worst thing a company can do is give no meaningful response.

Being customer-centric means that you have a two-way relationship built on trust. I'm going to work for you and you're going to be upfront with me. You're going to give me honest feedback when we're doing well and honest feedback when we're doing poorly. Not an easy approach to establish and maintain, but it is a prerequisite if you want to build a masterpiece.

So customer-centric behavior is a tough one for a lot of people, but we live and die by our NPS and CSAT scores each year because customers pay the bills. I was always proud of the fact that customers don't like our software; they love our software. But, as is inevitable with any product or service, there will be some things they don't like about your business model, your sales process, or your products. Yet we do our best to earn as must customer trust as we can.

Always remember—your customers are travelling along with you on your journey.

CHAPTER SEVEN ━━━━━━━━━

Building a Culture of Durability

Building a culture of durability—one that far outlasts the founder(s) or any one particular leader—is one of the greatest challenges in business. How do you hire skilled people? What skills are you looking for? What kinds of skills create a durable culture? Is emotional intelligence as important as technical competence? How do you identify problems, solve conflicts, and establish a workplace where respectful but frank feedback is the norm? Where everyone, including the CEO, is being held accountable for self-awareness, growth, and change? And what role do diversity and inclusion play in this equation?

In this chapter, I'll take a look at how I've experienced these issues throughout my career and at Alteryx in particular.

As I've made clear, facing, understanding, and mastering the emotional journey is crucial to any kind of success you'll have. We consciously integrate the emotional journey into our training and discussions. In our bootcamps, I often talk about the journey. I'll draw it on a whiteboard to let people know that my experience with Alteryx wasn't a straight line. And neither will their individual journeys with the company be straight lines.

I let them know that all of us go through the ups and downs of this journey. It's not a sign of weakness. It's not an indication of a character deficiency or a sign of moral failing.

I tell them that, sooner or later, their boss is going to ask them to prepare a report or an analysis.

"You'll think you've got a great idea, the best idea ever. And then your colleagues start taking potshots at it and you want to give up on the idea, maybe the job itself. A lot of people do that—they look for another role or transfer or quit altogether."

My role is to let them know it's not going to be a straight line. They have to drop that expectation. If they want to do great things, it's going to require many ups and downs.

While I believe leaders need to be transparent and vulnerable, I don't talk in very personal terms about my journey. I don't talk about the swamp of my divorce, for example. Sensible Socks and chimneyless fireplaces, yes, but nothing too personal. I don't have to reveal those kinds of experiences to help my employees recognize and navigate their particular peaks and valleys.

I make it clear that I wasn't a lucky guy who thought of an idea one day and found sudden success the next. The room lightens up. They have a laugh at my foibles. They realize the CEO is all too human. They understand that while there's risk involved, they too can get through the dark swamps to create a great career.

I inject humor as much as I can. I want them to know that if you can't laugh at yourself, then you're probably in the wrong company for sure. You can't take yourself too seriously. You've got to be able to laugh at yourself and admit that you've screwed up. You've got to be able to admit that you lack certain skills and need help from others.

An important part of our culture is keeping people on an even keel and not letting egos get out of control. The hubris of Silicon Valley drives me freaking crazy.

I learned as a child from dad that you've got to be humble when you're victorious. You need to learn from your defeats, not be humiliated by them. I want my teams to know this.

When we have a victory at Alteryx, you get a short period of time to celebrate it. You can't exult in your victory or chest-bump forever, so I instituted the "Sixty-Second Gloat Rule." If you win a big sale, you can ring the bell on the sales floor and scream and holler all you want—but only for 60 seconds. Then it's back to work because we have customers to support.

Over the years many people have come to talk to me about their careers, but just as many, if not more, have sought me out to discuss their emotional journeys. Leadership is in part predicated on your ability to be transparent, not only about the business end of things, but also about your strengths and failings and what you've learned along the way. Leadership is about humanizing the idea of what a leader should be.

As important as it is to hire people with good business sense, it's equally important, or even perhaps more so, to hire people with a high emotional quotient (EQ). EQ, also known as emotional intelligence, is the ability to understand, use, and manage your emotions in positive ways to relieve stress, communicate effectively, empathize with others, overcome challenges, and defuse conflict.

One way to talk about EQ versus IQ is "will" versus "skill." When we're interviewing, we can pretty quickly identify from the CV the skills that someone has. I don't spend as much time on skills interviewing as I do on EQ. I want to find out more about "will" than "skill."

I ask a range of questions about their backgrounds, their life experiences, and what motivates them. What do they read? What sports do they play? Is it a solo sport, like cycling, or a team sport? When someone says they play team sports, it's pretty telling. A team player has a greater sense of collaboration, of working as a unit, of helping out a teammate who might not be doing so well.

I also ask somewhat weird questions that help me understand the candidate's risk/reward profile. In a startup or growing business, you want people who aren't sheepish, who aren't afraid.

I almost always ask: "Have you ever started a business?" I frame the question by adding, "I'm not asking whether you were successful or not. I'm asking only to find out if you had the courage to start one."

A lot of people feel badly when they have to tell me that the business failed, but that's of zero concern to me.

"The most important part is you took the step," I say to them. "You had the courage to take a chance."

I'm not trying to find out whether or not they were successful in the traditional sense. I'm interested in what they learned (and learned not to do the next time). That's my definition of success. What did they learn from taking a risk? How did they respond to the risk/reward challenge? What would they do differently the next time?

I recently had a long conversation with a 26-year-old business development rep who had worked with us for the last year. He had sent me an email asking if he could meet to discuss his career. Of course, I told him. I'll always make time for that kind of discussion. I've always remembered the great swamp I was in, when I was going through my divorce and was ready to sell the company, with no one to talk to about my crisis. I will tirelessly help people to face and complete their journeys.

He knew I was approachable enough to have that conversation, and I loved hearing what he had to say. He said his ambition was to start a business. I would much rather have someone leave the company to start his or her own business than go to a competitor.

Every journey, no matter what it is, has a risk/reward profile, and that's why I admire people who start their own businesses: it's a high-risk venture that will likely become a long and emotional journey. When you look at the statistics of any journey, you need to be aware of your chances. You need to be realistic about the odds of success or failure you face.

The divorce rate among all marriages in the US is just under 50%, 60% for second marriages, and 71% for third marriages. College and high school graduation rates are quite dismal too. Nearly 20% of high schoolers never graduate and 40% of those who start their college journeys never complete them.

If you think these journeys are hard, let's take a look at business startups. There are about 500,000 startups every year. That's right—half a million people every year are stupid, naïve, foolish, OR courageous enough to take the big leap. And yet just 10% of those startups will survive the first five years of their journey. Only 72 out of every 10,000 new businesses will reach $6 million in revenue in six years, under 1%

of those that start. When I took Alteryx public in March 2017 there were roughly 4,000 public companies, and only 270 of them were software firms.

Facing risks and getting through the swamp have their rewards. In 2020, only 141 software companies did more than $450 million in annual recurring revenue (ARR). Alteryx did $493 million. Only 11 of those companies grew more than 30%. We grew at 32%. I think you get my point.

Knowing the risks shouldn't turn you away from your journey; instead, you can use risk and long odds as motivators to keep you on your game and to do your best work. Ignore WhatsApp as you're not likely to be like them. If you know that half of all marriages fail, you can choose not to get married. That's certainly a viable choice for many people. Or you can use that knowledge to really work at your marriage, to be proactive in addressing problems, in taking good care not to upset or hurt your partner in needless ways, and to develop the skills needed to be a better communicator.

Knowing the odds can scare people away from pursuing their dreams, but that awareness can also scare you straight, so to speak. If you are aware of the quagmire that could result if you're not careful, you're going to be more careful, more thoughtful, and more forward-thinking about your choices. Your eyes are wide open.

So it's a balance between having the guts and the courage to venture out, but at the same time also being mindful of the calculated risk. You need to have faith in a journey that is not yet known, but you should also have some sense of what you're getting into and not just rely on blind faith.

I recall talking to someone who is self-employed, a freelance writer. He was going through a rough period where the business wasn't going well. A friend put him in touch with someone who had also been a freelancer for years. "Give her a call," he said, "I think she can help."

So the freelancer called her up and the whole conversation was about having the right attitude. He was disappointed when he got off the phone because he had expected her to give him concrete help—people to call, leads to pursue, a particular strategy to employ.

She supplied none of that—her whole focus was on how to think positively about himself and have confidence.

He thought it was just fluff. But the more he reflected on what she said, the more he realized that she had given him the best possible advice. It wasn't about the nitty-gritty of how to run a business; it was all about mental attitude and managing emotions. Any success he had would flow from that. Will versus skill.

I ask salespeople interviewing for jobs if they own a boat. If they do, it's a sign that they play hard, which I like. And if they're a debt slave to the boat, which is usually the case, it means they're going to work hard to support the hobby. My son once confided in me that the second happiest day of his life was when he bought a boat—the happiest was when he sold it.

Another question I always ask when interviewing is, "We all have blind spots. What's yours?" A lot of candidates are very uncomfortable with that question as it requires a ton of self-awareness. If they say "I don't know," that's a huge red flag. It means they don't think they have any faults. People like this almost never make it through the dark swamps of despair in any journey they take.

They might be very empathetic, have great communication skills, and be self-motivated, but it's a huge blind spot if they don't think they have other work to do as well. We all have self-improvement work to do.

On the other hand, you might be willing to take the chance on someone who won't admit to a blind spot, as long as you can put them into a learning and development curriculum or assign them to a mentor to help raise their EQ.

Asking about blind spots is not the same as asking about ghosts, another of my favorite questions.

A blind spot is the admission of a skill you don't possess or a character flaw. If someone were to ask me about my blind spots, I'd say

I'm probably far too patient. That may sound counterintuitive for an entrepreneur of a fast-growth company, but it's true. When I try to help people improve or grow, I'm sometimes far too patient.

The ghost in the closet question is more of a way to understand not a weakness of character, but someone's ability to acknowledge and reveal the big things in their lives that make them uncomfortable. Talking about them is like stepping into a confessional at a Catholic church.

Ned, one of my co-founders, is in my view one of the most gifted software developers on the planet. I interviewed him for four months when considering him as our third co-founder. Finally, near the end of our discussions, I said to him: "Listen, Ned, I know that we all have ghosts in our closets. And my last question for you, before we either sign you up or part ways, is this: what is the ghost in yours?"

He became visibly nervous and blushed. He paused for a moment or two, avoiding eye contact.

"Well, when I was 12 years old, growing up in Greenwich, Connecticut, there was a knock on the door after I came home from school. I followed my mother, she opened the door, and there were two men in black suits and black ties."

"And who were they?" I asked.

"I loved coding and was curious about how far my skills might take me. Well, they caught me hacking into IBM's central accounting system, so I knew my skills could take me a long way. I was too young to get into serious trouble, and they simply wanted to find out how I did it so they could plug some holes."

I said to him, "Good, Ned, you're hired."

Why? I think there's something very powerful about someone who has the guts to do something like that and the honesty to reveal it.

Ned's admission told me he was creative and unafraid to try things most people wouldn't dare attempt. That's the kind of person I wanted in a startup.

In addition to being too patient, the ghost in my closet was that I was unwilling to work for other people. When I was young I worked for my father, which was fine. If I hadn't gone to college, I might have worked with him forever. But as I grew older I was really reluctant to work for other people, and maybe that was my ghost—being unwilling to learn from others. Maybe that's why the Alteryx journey took so long. I had to learn largely on my own as I went.

When I was young, I missed the opportunity to work a "regular job" as a burger flipper. In fact I'm kind of envious of my son, who worked for a hamburger stand named John's. He went and did it on his own, maybe because he didn't have the inclination initially to work with me (although, oddly enough, he ended up working with me at Alteryx for more than a decade). He took a "menial" job on his own initiative because he was interested in learning about the work world from others. He didn't have a problem being part of a team.

As a young and then an older father to my son, Reed.

Whenever I'm asked if I've regretted anything in my career, I suppose there are a few things I could moan about, but I've never really lamented much. There were painful moments for sure, but no failures. My only regret is not starting Alteryx sooner.

We lose sight of the fact that the journey is not linear and can be a very bumpy ride. The irony is that so many of the great minds, the great innovators, experienced repeated failure. That's why it's so important to develop the emotional strengths and personal strategies to get through the inevitable swamps.

In interviewing, I'm not looking for a single kind of emotional intelligence. For example, someone could be a very empathic individual but not a self-starter. They have a high EQ in one area yet lack an important trait for the job. You want people who are fairly outgoing because they have to communicate effectively with colleagues and clients.

If you're a big company, you might just be hiring in a targeted way, for a specific role. But if you're a growing company and need to build up the workforce, you have two choices. You can either promote from the inside or hire from the outside.

Promoting from the inside is the least disruptive, but it's also the hardest to do. This seems counterintuitive. Wouldn't it be easier to hire someone from the inside familiar with your business, versus someone who doesn't know your operations and culture? Yes, but hiring from the inside also has its risks. I often chuckle at my LinkedIn profile where people have endorsed me for skills I do not or will never possess. Anyone you promote from the inside has to be able to communicate in all directions, and many people who are promoted to leadership positions from within lack that skill.

If you need to go outside to find people with the exact skillset match, the challenge is that it can potentially be a culture disruptor to bring in someone who isn't currently in the club. For that reason insiders should get an equal, but not dominant, chance for promotions.

If you're in the mode of fast-paced growth, you might hire someone who can help get you to $1 billion in revenue, but that person might not have the EQ to get you to $5 billion.

I named Mark Anderson as my replacement when I stepped down as CEO in 2020. There were other people I suppose I could have chosen, but they had never seen a billion dollars in revenue. I said to the board, "I've got to find somebody who feels like me, talks like me, but who has gone down roads I've never gone down." I was fortunate to have found the ideal external candidate. And having been on our board of directors for two years, Mark had a running head start.

And so you have to go outside to fill some positions. If you want to do it from inside, you have to skill them up to be able to get from $10 million to $50 million, or from no direct reports to 10 direct reports, or from 10 direct reports to a hundred direct reports. And if they're aware of their blind spots and have identified their EQ weaknesses, you can put them into a learning program well in advance to address their deficiencies.

One of the most important things you can do to build a durable culture is have career counseling discussions with new hires on the day they start. You might have hired them to immediately fill a major void, but if you don't understand their wants and ambitions, as well as their weaknesses and blind spots, you'll eventually have to replace them. And that to me is no way to build a strong and sustainable culture.

We should help each other identify each other's blind spots and train each other to overcome them. One of the greatest gifts we have is the "360 Performance Review," where you're evaluated not just by your boss, but by the peers you work with every day.

Many of us are afraid to get these reviews because we don't want to hear bad news. I tell my employees that a 360 Review is a gift, the best thing you could ever do for yourself, because you're going to find out how other people see you. It's very hard to see yourself objectively, but it can change your life. The 360 allows you to see your strengths and weaknesses through the eyes of others. It can be painful to hear about your blind spots, but it's a good and necessary kind of pain if you're going to gain in self-awareness and emotional maturity. It can be a great corrective tool, and that's why we conduct 360 Reviews regularly with staff.

Another way to get revealing feedback is to write down on a piece of paper all the things you're good at and all the things you're bad at. Then have your spouse or partner or child or deepest friend make the same list about you. Those two lists are not likely to be the same, but they will also be profoundly instructive.

This kind of reflection is an especially important process for anyone who you believe has leadership potential—someone who can captivate an audience, who can articulate the complex in a simplified way and have people get it, or communicate complex things in an intelligent way to an engineering team and have them get it. To me, those are really important skills.

When a leader tells me she has gotten along with her core team for the last five years, I think that's unfortunate. Why? Because she hasn't been challenged by the people she leads. She hasn't had to look at her blind spots. If you're a good salesperson the assumption is that you will be a good sales leader, but when promoted into field leadership positions most salespeople don't do well. Leadership requires another level of skills, but without a review process from peers you can't determine whether or not you have them.

Recently I talked with an employee who was trying to navigate today's cancel culture with his team.. He was facing pushback from more progressive team members who didn't like his conservative ideas.

"I don't really want to talk with them about my values," he told me.

"Well, you should show up as the authentic and best version of yourself," I said, "including talking about your values. Just don't push them on others. State your values and beliefs honestly and openly, and don't dismiss other people's values and beliefs in the process." Inclusion and diversity in action.

"Should I talk to them about my faith?"

"Well, you can, just be aware that you might turn some people off."

Good leaders have the ability to use language to convey how they live their lives without dismissing how other people live their lives. I don't really talk about my Christian faith at work, but I've often said that while I grew up Catholic—my higher power is always looking out for me—our family also took detours from Catholicism. Instead of going to church on Sunday, our family of seven went to a restaurant and ate and talked for three hours. It was phenomenal.

And there are many ways to have this kind of communication within a corporate culture.

I got a text the other day from a woman on our engineering teams. She said, "Thinking back to our conversation from months ago, I've now gotten the entrepreneurial spirit."

And that's the legacy I want. Not that I built Alteryx into a multi-billion-dollar company. To me, that's irrelevant. What's more relevant is how many great leaders I helped produce. When someone says that a conversation with me years ago encouraged her to start a business or change careers or ask for a promotion, I love that. That goes even for someone who moves on and becomes a great leader somewhere else.

On the opening day at bootcamp, I say, "Most of you won't be here in five years and that's too bad. I wish you would stay here. And I hope we can make this a great home for you, but I understand people need to make life changes and career changes. You might move to another city and we may not have a job for you there. Or you might not like your role here. And we might not like what you're doing here.

"I never will discourage you from leaving, but I *will* discourage you from going to another company for the wrong reasons. Make sure you're running *to* a company, not running *from* a company. And if you're running from this company, either we've done something terribly wrong in trying to help you in your career, or you've done something terribly wrong to not help yourself."

Years ago I had a debate with my then CFO about investing in employee learning and development. "Gary, when we bring in new employees, we're gonna spend a ton of money training them. We're going to get their careers on track. We're going to educate them, give them scholarships, and do whatever it takes to make them great."

And he said, "That's a bad idea."

"Why?"

"Well, what if we spend all this money training them and they leave?"

And I replied, "But what if we don't and they stay?"

Another major foundation in building a culture of durability is creating a diverse, inclusive, and equitable workplace. I developed a healthy respect for diversity as a 20-year-old college senior at CU Boulder, when I had the chance to spend over three months travelling around the world in a program called Semester at Sea. It was a spectacular adventure. In almost every country we visited, I had experiences that led me to the realization that we're all part of the same humanity, that pretty much all of us long for the same thing. But how we get there is going to be unique for each of us.

Having circumnavigated the globe some 35,000 miles, the last city we visited was Dakar, Senegal, in French-speaking West Africa. We toured the 88-acre island of Goree, or in French, Île de Gorée. We visited jail cells, where hundreds of years ago the slave trade with America began. As I watched a ceremony there, I thought about the African people who wanted something great and who were instead enslaved. How their dreams, for centuries, became a swamp of despair. They wanted only what you or I wanted, and yet they were denied that fundamental dream, their basic humanity. And, as recent events have made indelibly clear, the cost of that injustice resonates to this day.

In Durban, South Africa, I encountered the peak of apartheid. I saw black kids being bused into the city at 5:00 a.m. to work for white people.

"I'm just trying to put food on the table for my family," one nervous young man said to me, because talking to a white guy was a line you did not cross without consequences.

I visited Lake Nakuru in Kenya, famous for the biggest flamingo flock in the world. Unfortunately I got there three days late, so there were no flamingos. One night I didn't lock the door to my motel room, even though we were in the middle of freaking nowhere. In walks a Kenyan who reaches into my suitcase and steals my Denver Nuggets basketball shirt. I kind of pretended I was asleep because I had no idea what would happen if he knew I saw him.

The next day the tour leaders and local authorities made a federal case out of it. They wanted me to identify him in a lineup, but I declined to do so. I had the realization that he was on a journey, too. He just needed clothes to travel along it. I was happy to oblige.

When I left Dakar, it was a seven-day voyage back to Fort Lauderdale, Florida. Looking out over the vast ocean, I kept thinking about the range of peoples and cultures and customs I had been witness to, but apart from those outward differences I knew we had much more in common.

It was a seminal moment for me, but I couldn't explain this insight to anyone when I returned. If I had said, "At the most fundamental level, we're all the same," I would have gotten blank stares.

Has Dean been smoking something?

But I felt the truth of it in my bones then, and still do to this day.

My parents had healthy discussions with us about our personal life strategies. What journey would we be going on when we went off to college? What were our individual ambitions? What were the family's ambitions? What did we have to do collectively to get there? What personal commitments would we have to make?

We had equitable discussions that were focused on being positive. We haggled, we debated, and sometimes we argued pretty hard, but after all that we came back together and we broke bread.

After the meal was over dad would draw straws, and whoever had the shortest one would have to get on their bike and ride to the local convenience store, about two and a half blocks away, with instructions to pick up two or three candy bars. Dad cut them into seven pieces, one for each of us.

We may have had disagreements about schoolwork, or our ambitions for college, or about what was going on in dad's business, but our conversations almost always ended in this fair and equitable way where everyone still felt heard and recognized. While we might not have gotten exactly what we wanted, we always got what we needed. The Stoecker household epitomized equity and inclusion.

The framework to address this issue today, in the corporate world, is inclusion and diversity.

Although we live in a cancel culture, our differences are what give us strength. Beneath those differences, we all share a common bond. We all want to provide for our families. We all want to have a great marriage. We all want to build relationships. I was fortunate to have an insight into this before starting the business. I couldn't explain it to people. But after Alteryx became successful and I travelled around the world to set up offices in 13 countries, I began to relive that experience at sea. That's when I began to realize how huge an impact it had on me. I couldn't explain it then, but I could now.

I recall being in Brazil on business, and during a cab ride my wife and I were talking about politics. The driver was very tuned into the conversation.

He said to us, "Well, it's good to know that you're also worried about your government. We have a corrupt one here in Brazil, and I have to figure out how to protect my family from it."

It hit me again. We have the same dreams—a good job, food on the table, a roof over our heads, a better life for our children.

This understanding should be the foundation of our diversity and inclusion programs.

I've always believed that you want the best person for the job. And if it's a tie between two people, and one is African-American or Hispanic or Asian or LGBTQ, you pick that person. What makes us strong is when we bring not varied colors, religions, or ethnicities to the table, but varied experiences. Identities don't define us but experiences certainly do.

A lot of companies, tech companies especially, employ primarily men who build products used by women. Diversity and customer-centric behavior overlap right there.

We recognize that our software is used in every industry for the craziest stuff—from the Green Bay Packers using it to run player analytics, to doing derivatives modeling on Wall Street, to optimizing retail shelf spaces, to alerting NASCAR drivers about when they should make a pit stop.

At Alteryx, we know that the users of our products are diverse. They're in 90-plus countries. They speak many languages. They're men, women, LGBTQ, and just about every race and ethnicity. Supporting them and building great products for them demands diversity in the way we build those products, and that means having a full spectrum of people on our teams, including in the C-suite and on the board of directors.

Perhaps the best examples of the need for gender diversity in business are in product development. Consider that, less than a decade ago, women drivers had a 47% greater chance of serious injury in a crash than their male counterparts, in part because, until 2012, the design for car crash dummies was based on an average male body. Some smartphone features, as well as the size of the device itself, appear to be designed for larger male hands rather than the smaller hands of women. And then there's the Apple Watch, which was designed with several health and fitness features when it debuted in 2015, but didn't include menstrual cycle tracking until four years later—several product models after it came out.

I'd be willing to bet that the design teams for many of these products were largely comprised of men.

One of our customers, Patrick Emmanuelle, worked as an analyst for TBC Corporation in Florida, one of the world's largest marketers and distributors of automobile tires.

I said to him once, "Patrick, what do you think of our software?"

And he had the most remarkable response.

"I love Alteryx, Dean, because it rewards me for the way I think."

That's not what you typically see in most enterprise software, where the users have to adapt the way they work to the "buttonology" that's provided. With our software, you can adapt our technology to the way *you* work and the way *you* think. You can make it *your* software.

And that's fun and gratifying to witness.

As a company, we recognize that we're incredibly diverse in the way our software is used, in our customer base, in the range of cultures we sell to. So it would be a big mistake if we were a predominantly white male development company. We've tried very hard to make sure that we have a great mixture of races, cultures, religions, personalities, and backgrounds.

When I first started in business, I was selling Equal Employment Opportunity Commission (EEOC) data back when the government enforced Title VII of the Civil Rights Act of 1964. Companies had to hire a requisite ratio of black, Latino, or female engineers. In short, there was a hiring quota. I didn't like selling the data because I felt it didn't give my customers a better business; it just made them compliant with a regulation.

I was trying to convince people that I had the data that would help them create a more successful business. Then they would have the resources to hire a truly diverse staff and not just fill a quota.

What makes a business better is bringing in diversity of *experiences*. And you generally get that when you have diversity in your workforce in race, gender, and sexual orientation.

We still want the skill. But if someone has the requisite skills for what we need to do, by all means we take diversity into account. And I know it makes us a lot stronger.

So I put together a diversity and inclusion program called Alter. US that includes all kinds of employee resource groups—a BIPOC group for employees of color and indigenous people, an ERG for women (Women and Allies), and an ERG for military veterans and many more. It gives people comfort knowing that as a company we're thinking about the right thing.

I want to be remembered not as the guy who hit a particular sales number, but as someone who helped my team build their careers, work in a diverse and supportive culture, and start a new business if they so choose. And that's true for every one of our 1,600 associates around the world today.

CHAPTER EIGHT

True Leaders Build Leaders, Not Followers

Social media gets it all wrong. I recall reviewing my LinkedIn profile a few years back. I had lots of followers and connections, but many were endorsing me for skills I don't even possess. There was no connection between why they were following me and who I really was. It renewed my belief that leadership isn't about how many followers you have and what they say about you. That can be incredibly superficial. It's about how many new leaders you create and what *they* do with the skills you've taught them.

I learned this truth in childhood. My father wasn't just a great dad. He was a great leader because he made his five kids great leaders. All of my siblings have been quite successful in either building a family or a business or a career. And I give my parents enormous credit for that.

You never entirely grasp the example your parents are setting while you're growing up. Why is mom asking me to get on my knees and pray with her? Why do we have to eat dinner as a family? Why do we have to do chores and share responsibilities?

Only later on in life did I realize that I was being taught the building blocks of creating anything great—discipline, humility, humbleness, hard work, and persistence.

All of us with mom
(from left to right: Dean, John, Robin, Steve, and Kathy).

During my journey at Alteryx, I realized that I had to institute learning and development programs to upskill the work force, if we were going to create something great. You have to hire people who not only have good business ideas and competencies, but who have emotional intelligence and competencies. And you have to help them improve their emotional competency, their ability to handle the ups and downs, the inevitable swamps that will come their way.

What prompted this? My biggest fear was that I didn't have leaders who I had developed from within the company, and I knew that I couldn't be the only storyteller if we were going to scale. The reason I instituted leadership programs was to identify and develop talent from within. I was going to help anyone who wanted to become a better leader. Leaders build leaders.

I didn't want to be the kind of CEO who had to call all the shots. I didn't want it to be all about me, with no one else involved in decision making. In order to make that happen, I wanted to make sure that I developed leaders who were thoughtful, who carefully evaluated risk and tried to mitigate as much of it as possible in the shortest period of time, so we could grab opportunity and make stuff happen.

My first foray into leadership training was to hire the Franklin Covey organization out of Salt Lake City, founded by Stephen Covey, author of the highly influential leadership book, *The Seven Habits of Highly Effective People.*

I handpicked people in the company to attend the intensive training—people who had leadership titles, but who I wasn't sure were actually effective leaders. Title inflation occurs in companies, just like grade inflation in college. I also selected people who had said they wanted to be leaders someday. And in other cases I saw glimmers of talent in workers who weren't in leadership positions. They had finesse, the ability to dissect problems and solve them, but their skills had been overlooked. I took this group and put them through three days of Franklin Covey training.

The result?

Mostly a huge disappointment. The training was good, but it didn't result in strong leaders.

Some people in our company were book-smart but street-stupid, and the Franklin Covey training didn't seem to have an impact on this. After three days of group discussions, roleplaying, and problem solving, one of my engineers said to me, "Dean, I don't really understand why the revenue goal is important." Another one of my top people jumped in and said, "I don't understand it either."

I thought, *Wow. I just spent 20 grand putting them through three days of leadership training, and that's the most compelling question they have?*

For me, *The Seven Habits* boiled down into two realizations that were most critical for Alteryx's success, and my ability to both lead people and build leaders:

1) People need to have an acute understanding of strategies, and

2) people need the ability to identify tactically what needs to be done for that strategy to come to fruition.

And that is very hard to do.

When someone says, "I just don't understand why revenue's important," they believe that if you simply build it they will come, but I can guarantee you that's not the case for most companies. You have to sell stuff, market stuff, and service stuff; and while you can't have just a profit-minded organization, especially in today's world with ESG and idealistic, social justice oriented millennials, you have to make money to be able to give back.

I want to give back, too, but first you have to do more than give back. You've got to pay your bills. You've got to make payroll. You've got to reinvest to keep the machine running in order to keep the customers—the bill payers—happy.

I was stunned by that statement. In fact, the woman who taught the class was stunned too. She looked at me with an expression that said, "Oh my God, we just spent three days talking about the importance of strategy, tactics, and the Seven Habits, and someone wonders why revenue is important?"

And so my response was, "Well, why don't I stop paying you? And then you tell me why revenue is important."

The left-brain folks think everything will take care of itself. And if that happens, the revenue is just going to come in and we don't have to worry about it.

Idealistic thinking—I can focus on what I like to do, not necessarily what is required to be done.

But if you're an entrepreneur and a strong leader, you have to drive your team to hit the numbers. And to do that, you've got to write code that makes customers excited. The point is, a lot of people have trouble seeing the relationship between strategy and tactics. And for any success in anything, you have to do both well. These are universal lessons here that apply to a lot of situations in life.

After a few years of using the Steven Habits, I realized that I needed leadership training that more directly applied to the challenges we faced.

More than identifying potential new leaders, the Franklin Covey training exposed weaknesses in people who were already in leadership positions.

I knew I had to surround these weaker leaders with stronger people. The training gave me an opportunity to weed out those people who were too early in their careers to become strong leaders. It enabled me to identify those who weren't good, critical thinkers and who didn't have high emotional intelligence.

We've been conducting leadership development programs for many years now. We put existing leaders through difficult real-world tasks within the company, which we've found to be the most effective, real-world approach, not academic or theoretical. We give them two or three challenging subjects that we've faced at Alteryx and they spend three or four months dissecting them, to understand what's working and what's not working. They present their analysis and solutions to leadership, which helps us determine who we want rowing the boat.

And yet my biggest fear, even to this day, is not having enough quality leaders within the company.

One of the weaknesses in many leaders is their inability to communicate within the company. I always tell my leaders that they've got to sell downstream in the company, not just up and laterally. We can converse for days about great strategies and tactics that we're going to implement, but if we don't communicate those strategies and tactics to our teams, the people who have to execute them, then nothing happens. Too often this communication doesn't happen. Leadership isn't about trying to impress Dean, I tell my leaders. It's about influencing and motivating the people who report to you.

The most valuable communication is the downward conversation. Whenever you hear someone say about a leader, "That person's political," it's probably because they can bullshit their boss. What they can't do is articulate the "why" and the "what" to their own teams.

The magic happens with the teams, not in the C-suite. The magic happens with leaders who are able to sit down with the people who are building things and writing things and supporting things and taking care of the business. If you can't articulate to someone why they should be doing a certain kind of work, then why would they want to do it? At that point they're just a drone.

Why do leaders fail to communicate with their teams?

People get impressed with titles and think they only need to communicate laterally with other leaders. I tell my team that when you're done meeting with the big boss, you need to put together a team meeting or a town hall. You need to go through a deck describing what we talked about and what was resolved, what has to be done, and how your teams are involved in executing the plan.

I got very good at identifying who was good at this and who was not. When tactical items fell off the screen, I knew immediately which leaders hadn't done a good job of communicating strategy.

As a leader, I've focused on three fundamental principles, and the first is be concerned about my employees' ambitions. What would they like to be known for? What potential career path will get them there? What do they need to do to be successful on that path?

The second fundamental principle is to be a servant leader. I like to let my workers shadow me whenever that's possible. That way they can actually witness and understand how decisions are made, rather than me handing them down as a *fait accompli*. By shadowing me, they can help me understand ways to make better decisions. They can improve decisions I've made or teach me new approaches. I can learn from them. And to me, that's servant leadership.

The third principle is to acknowledge that as your career becomes more successful, as your journey bears fruit, your role as a leader is not to know more about more, but rather less and less about more. The more you rise in stature and skill as a leader, the more you should be handing off responsibility and leadership to others. You should be preparing to hand off the ball so others can run the show.

I told investors years before going public that my biggest challenge would be building a corporate culture that would help the company thrive in perpetuity. And that's really hard to do because each of us has our particular goals, expectations, values, belief systems, and life experiences.

And so we've tried to define and build a culture where people can have their differences, but in the end have a common bond and are focused on the same mission. That common bond transcends their differences. Again, not an easy thing to do.

Companies often develop cultures that are detrimental to their well-being and sustainability. Sometimes the founder has trouble letting go. The organization has to go from being the founder's baby to becoming an organization that can stand on its own feet, not bound by the founder's cultural attitudes.

I have found it very easy to step aside and turn it over to someone else. At the first board of directors meeting following our IPO, one of my board members said to me, "Dean, you've led the company for over 20 years. How long are we going to have you?" I learned that succession planning is one of the most critical things a public company CEO must do.

I said, "As long as you need me."

"Well, don't you want to be around when we hit a billion dollars in revenue?"

I was a quarterback in high school and had a lot of success on the field, because to me the heroes were the guys who ran it into the end zone or caught the long pass. Letting someone else take over and run the last 25 yards was extremely gratifying. It meant the march down the field was well conceived and executed.

"I don't think I need to be around," I said, "because I'll have built a foundation where someone who's talented can just pick it up and run. I actually think it's more gratifying to be able to hand it off to someone else and make sure they have a clear shot at the end zone."

I really didn't care about the financial milestone. Too much of leadership is wound up in the "me" as opposed to the "you."

This requires a lot of emotional intelligence, which I've had to work at as hard as anyone else. The work is crucial. So many of our state and national leaders have been caught up in scandals of one kind or another. We read about horrendous management styles that result in toxic, even abusive work environments.

These aren't servant leaders. A servant leader doesn't try to undermine or destroy his or her critics. Instead, a servant leader seeks out the advice of critics to learn how to be a better leader. I want my fellow workers to tell me where I've gone wrong. Don't forget—when you're in the swamp you'll need all the help you can get.

Relationships present the same kind of challenges and opportunities. If you're doing more listening than talking (either to your partner or to yourself), you're on the right track. When you sit down with your kids around the dinner table, it's not dad talking about what dad did. It's dad asking the kids what they learned in school that day. It's mom asking about their aspirations and goals, their hopes and dreams.

If you can welcome feedback and respond to it positively and not with defensiveness, you will then have a good chance of growing and moving forward. These are the kinds of conversations I have with my associates. What are your goals? What goals do we share? How are we going to reach our goals together?

Solid marriages are based on both partners being transparent about what they want to accomplish and then helping each other to reach those goals. It can't be about "me." The best marriage or relationship will hit the swamp eventually. And you end up there not because of sex or money troubles; you end up there because of a failure to communicate. When the honeymoon ends, both parties have to figure out if they want to get through the muck and, if so, how to come out the other end in one piece. It can't be done alone.

And if you can't get through it, you can still have a positive outcome. I've got two beautiful, strong, and smart (EQ and IQ) kids who figured out how to get through their parents' divorce. They're living their own journeys now and they're engaged in life to its fullest.

I imagine my father was thinking the same things at this point is his life, after my siblings and I left home. He was probably asking himself: did I do a good job? Are my kids achieving the dreams and desires and ambitions that we talked about around the dinner table?

As a CEO, you have to wait until the public investors and your target market "get you." As a parent, you have the same wait: when will the kids finally "get us?" Some of us have to wait until our kids are out of the house before they can say, "I love you."

Oh, he finally gets me.

To be a strong leader, collaboration is critical. I put people into groups during our training sessions and observe them. If they don't participate, if they're quiet during the conversation, it tells me they probably aren't the ones to motivate a team of people from diverse backgrounds in a functional area of the business, and certainly not cross-functional teams. They aren't the ones to forge a collaborative, problem-solving approach.

This is why I moved away from the Franklin Covey events; they were instructive but a little too academic. We started doing programs internally that were more related to the real-world problems we faced.

One team, the emerging leaders team, would be tasked with solving strategic problems. For example, the company needs a certain kind of technology to run more efficiently. Go develop an assessment of what technology you might buy or partner with, and fold it into Alteryx to drive that efficiency gain.

Or we'd give them a more tactical problem—a known problem

that we had identified but struggled to solve. Go solve this problem and present back your findings and recommendations.

The goal was to make sure the strategic thinkers were tactically adept, and that the tactically skilled could learn how to think strategically. We wanted them to achieve that critical balance.

At Alteryx we give you a 14-day free trial of our software ("Trial to Win"), but we were having difficulties converting trials into sales. Over a couple of years a bunch of people tried to solve it in various ways, but nobody was really thinking about it as an end-to-end process. So the emerging leaders team was tasked with finding a strategic solution to the problem, instead of just running a bunch of numbers and reporting back how bad things were or what the opportunities might be with a process fix.

When I say that my biggest fear is not having leaders, we have to remember that most people aren't natural born leaders.

It's pretty much a fact today (first discovered way back during the IBM growth days) that the appropriate span of control should be no more than seven. In other words, if you're going to hire 700 people, you've got to have 100 leaders to manage them. If you're going to grow from 500 employees to 1,200, the chances of finding a hundred leaders out of your current 500 employees to manage that growth are going to be slim.

To meet that demand, you either have to hire externally or figure out how to up-skill existing leadership. And we saw some great success in doing the latter.

One of our leaders, Jim Schattin, comes to mind. He was with us for 15 years, joining us in 2005 as a product manager and sole contributor. He hit a few swamps, and there were times it seemed he was barely going to get through them, but we helped him come out the other end.

When he left the company, he had close to 400 people reporting to him. He was empathic and a great listener. He never asked his team to do something he wasn't willing to do. He was the hardest worker, the most engaged, and that set a superlative example.

He understood that if you could get your team to understand strategy correctly, you'll have a much greater success in tactical execution. The usual approach is to do a bunch of work without any overall direction and hope you're heading the right way. That is not an efficient or effective way of operating.

He left the company as a senior vice president of customer success and went on to be a chief customer officer at a smaller, fast-growing tech company. I'm proud of the fact that he left us for a great opportunity. I could have lamented his leaving, but I was so happy for him.

Too many leaders have a chip on their shoulders. They think leadership is sitting in an office, barking orders, and watching everyone dutifully follow them. But if you can't articulate to your team why something should be done instead of demanding it be done, then you shouldn't be a leader.

It's very easy to determine who's a good leader or not. If you ask someone if they've ever done a 360 Review with their team and they say no, it's generally because they either didn't know they existed or are afraid of the feedback. That leads to hubris, which can have far more devastating effects than overpriced art objects in the lobby.

I think the founder of Uber tainted almost all high-tech leaders with his horrible behavior in the company, whether in regard to inclusion and diversity or behavior with women in the workforce. The board ended up tossing him out. The ultimate 360.

And then there's Jack Dorsey. I'm not a fan of Twitter.

There are good people in Silicon Valley who build great businesses and help people in their careers and lives. And there are people who give back, like Benioff from Salesforce.

But this last generation of tech leaders got caught up in themselves, thinking their ideas were better than anyone else's, beating their chests about becoming unicorns. It drives me crazy because business success isn't about achieving a market cap level. It's about serving your customers and treating your employees with fairness and respect. This is what drives the value of businesses.

On the night of our IPO, Mark told me we changed his family's life—that's what executives should be focused on. And when someone says why worry about revenue, I say let's worry about changing lives. When you are successful at this, you drive revenue.

You've got to be humble in your victories and show humility in your defeats. And I've always kept my father in mind, how he lashed out at me only once in all the years I worked for him. He didn't take out his defeats or disappointments on anyone. He was the most humble, the most gracious man I've ever met. And after working his tail off each week, he would spend Saturday afternoon at the Sister Carmen Center, packing food bags for people in need. If he missed a day, he always made it up by adding two extra days the next week. His discipline in giving was remarkable. I recently came across his handwritten spreadsheet where he kept track of his weekly tithing at Holy Trinity Catholic Church. It was not about the amounts he gave, it was about the regularity.

DATE	AMOUNT	TO
1-1-57 ✓	.25	St. Catherines
1-6-57 ✓	1.10	Holy Ghost
1-11-57 ✓	.50	March of Dimes
1-13-57 ✓	1.70	Holy Ghost
1-20-57 ✓	1.00	Our Lady
1-27-57 ✓	1.30	St. Dominic's
1-28-57 ✓ Don't count on Tax	1.00	(Max Crum's Mother) Office Collection
2-3-57 ✓	.85	Holy Ghost
2-10-57 ✓	ABSENT	Sick
2-17-57 ✓	1.70	Holy Ghost
2-24-57 ✓	.60	Holy Ghost
3-3-57 ✓	.70	Holy Ghost
3-10-57 ✓	1.55	Holy Ghost
3-17-57 ✓	1.60	Holy Ghost
3-24-57 ✓	ABSENT	Flat Tire
3-31-57 ✓	1.45	Holy Ghost

Dad kept a meticulous record of his donations to the church.

All CEOs and entrepreneurs need to be servant leaders.

Most companies don't deal well with the human side of the equation, how people get along and work together. It's a big reason why many companies don't survive.

I was having a discussion about the business recently with my new CEO, who stepped into an $8 billion market cap company as a first-timer.

I said to him, "In this role, you're going to have to figure out a way to humanize yourself to our workforce." Many executives find that impossible to do, especially those from the Baby Boomer generation who grew up or worked under more authoritarian kinds of parents and leaders. But being human and vulnerable are crucial to being a good leader.

It's always amusing to me how people react to job titles, which is usually based on their experience with other people who've had that title. I remember flying to London for an event and our VP of marketing in London, whom I had never met, sent me an email as I was getting on the airplane:

> *I need to get you a driver and a security guard when you get to London.*

So I wrote back: *Why would we do that?*

She replied: *All the CEOs I've worked for do that.*

And I told her: *That's not me. I will get a driver and a security guard when you do.*

I was in the office the other day, picking up my mail, and ran into a gentleman named Philip Jones who runs our sales operations team. Due to COVID I hadn't seen anybody in the office for literally a year, and that's why I stopped and said hello.

"Dean, how have you been since retiring?"

"I've been really good."

"I don't know if you recall what I asked you in my final interview, before I joined the company."

I said, "I'm sorry, I don't."

He said, "Well, I told you I had worked for a bunch of seasoned

Silicon Valley CEOs. And I said that if you were like them, I'd be sorry to come work for you."

Philip laughed and then added, "But you weren't like them at all. You're always a pleasure to work with."

It was one of the highest compliments I've ever been paid.

But while leadership is not about being authoritarian, neither is it about democracy.

Years ago I found in a magazine a saying that I photocopied and framed. I've referred to it often, whenever I feel a swamp approaching or am caught in one.

> IF YOU WANT TO SEE SOMETHING done, just tell some human beings it can't be done. Make it known that it's impossible to fly to the moon, or run a hundred metres in nine-point-nine seconds, or solve Fermat's Last Theorem. Remind the world that no one has ever hit sixty-two home runs in a season. Stuffed eighteen people into a Volkswagen Bug. Set half the world free. Or cloned a sheep. Dangle the undoable in front of the world. Then, consider it done.

This quote hung on my wall for years. Still does.

Leadership is about motivating ordinary humans to do extraordinary things. You can't do that by having a weekly sit-down on performance reviews. And you certainly can't accomplish it by barking orders from your corner office. You have to lead from the front and encourage, inspire, and, when you need to, even push from behind.

CHAPTER NINE

My Art of War: Timeless Lessons on Strategy and Tactics

In 2004 I began our ritual of Bing Fa—monthly, quarterly, and annual executive alignment sessions to discuss strategy and tactics, using the framework provided by Sun Tzu's *The Art of War*. It provided us with an opportunity for debate, through which we could find alignment and accountability in how we operated. It allowed us to evaluate and renew Alteryx's leadership culture. Bing Fa was the corporate version of the dinner table discussions I had had with my family years before.

What Bing Fa really means is subject to debate. Some scholars translate it as "methods for using soldiers." It usually refers to the use of military strategy in war.

But according to scholar David G. Jones, that's a misunderstanding of Sun Tzu's work.

> [A] careful reading of *The Art of War* shows it is not at all about war. The title is in fact a mistranslation of *Bing-Fa*, a 2,300-year-old expression that means "the art of diplomacy." Or the more accurate translation, "the art of managing organizations and relations between organizations."

However it's translated, Bing Fa is about the deployment and use of forces, with a key tenet of also conserving them—how you use your people most effectively and most efficiently, without going to war. Sun Tzu wrote:

> To win one hundred victories in one hundred battles is not the acme of skill. To subdue the enemy without fighting is the acme of skill.

It's about understanding the skills that are required to prevail in a conflict, and to know what to do in the event of a fight. It's about making sure that strategy and tactics are perfectly aligned, probably the hardest thing to do in business. It was certainly very hard for me to do at Alteryx.

We held our first Bing Fa meeting in November 2004. At the time we had a big effort around building and integrating our products into a platform, devising plans to migrate from an on-premises solution to a cloud and hybrid solution. We tried to build in as much flexibility as possible because we didn't really know how the market was going to react, how long it would take, or what use cases it might be adopted for, initially or further into the future. We had to cushion ourselves in the event that our timing was off, or if the market we were going after was the wrong one, or if the customer we thought we should be selling to weren't the right ones.

In so doing I learned that my team struggled with committing to either strategy or tactics.

It was frustrating because sometimes we were good at strategy and bad at tactics. Other times we were bad at strategy and great at tactics. We couldn't find alignment between the two and it is that alignment that is most critical. I tried to get my team to understand my construct for improving alignment, but this one was too big. The strategy and tactics conundrum was the cornerstone of being successful, but I couldn't find a way to frame or communicate it. I thought an intensive company-wide immersion in *The Art of War* would provide the framework to help with this dilemma.

For as Sun Tzu writes:

> Strategy without tactics is the slowest route to victory. Tactics without strategy is the noise before defeat.

This became the mantra for Bing-Fa. For me, this insight was revolutionary. It provided a framework for identifying and rectifying problems we were having. It explained why we failed to make progress in certain areas after great meetings. I realized we were failing to think strategically first. What were we trying to accomplish and why? What was most important to us? Where was the market heading? What customer needs were we trying to meet next year? In the next five years? The next ten years?

And once we agreed on our forward strategy, what tactics did we need to employ to make the strategy work? What did the company leaders have to do? What did each of our teams need to do? What kinds of training or protocols did we have to employ? What human and investment capital was needed?

This framework applies to many other journeys in life. If you're not getting along with your partner or your kids, what strategically do you want to accomplish in this relationship? What's the big picture? You can't lose sight of that, which often happens. And once you see the big picture and have established your goals, what specific steps will you take to reach them?

The strategy and tactics division can be a nice way of looking at conflicts in any kind of relationship. For example, you're bogged down in tactics if your only goal is to win an argument with someone. If your strategy is to maintain a relationship that matters to you, that tactic is short-sighted. But if your sole focus is maintaining the relationship without taking specific steps to do so, you have a strategy without teeth, one that can't be executed.

If you're having problems in a relationship, you lose sight of what you need to do to keep it going. You assume it's going along fine when it's not, when it's a fragile creature that requires constant understanding and attention.

I can remember having a debate with my first wife when cell phones started taking off. She wanted our son to have a phone as soon as possible. I wasn't so sure, worried that he was headed toward social illiteracy if his phone became his best friend. It was a little thing that we disagreed about, along with many other things. It's not necessarily just the big things that swamp you in the journey.

I can recall asking each of my kids a bunch of times, "What do you want?"

"I want that bicycle."

"What do you think you're going to have to do to get it?"

If they couldn't answer that question, I wanted them to understand that the bicycle wouldn't be arriving any day soon.

At the initiation of Bing Fa we were still relatively small, approaching $6 million in revenue and 30 employees, and I understood that as we got bigger, every move we made would become more critical. The opportunities would be greater, but so would the downside. The need to align strategies with tactics was urgent.

I don't remember how I initially stumbled across Sun Tzu. I might have searched in Google for "strategic alignment" or something like that. I read part of his original work and found it very hard to understand.

There have been dozens of make-overs of *The Art of War*—for leadership, business, management, etc. I picked up one that had a business translation of the original.

Some of his sayings were spot-on for what I was thinking and feeling at that moment. For example, he said that if you don't have resources, the best way to win a war is to not go into battle. You have to be efficient with your expenditures, knowing what to spend money on and what not to.

This resonated with me because there were so many competitors in our space. It's still true today, but back then there were a lot of players much bigger than us. The waters were filled with sharks and we'd get eaten if we weren't careful.

Sun Tzu's checklist includes deception. When you're weak, you have to act strong. And when you're strong, you have to act weak. As you've seen, I put the art of deception into practice quite often in my journey, and at this point I found opportunities to use it again.

If we developed something that was super disruptive, we didn't talk about it. If we had something that wasn't very unique or powerful, we talked up how great it was. We were very selective about what information we revealed. We didn't intentionally deceive people, but sometimes we led them into thinking we were stronger than we were, so we could keep competitors at bay until we could financially contend with them. We dodged some bullets, but our strategy and tactics were still woefully unaligned.

In 2004 I sent the following email to my team.

Sent: Sunday, September 19, 2004

Subject: Bing-Fa Summit

Hi guys:

That's right, Bing-Fa. It is the Chinese translation of what we know as Sun Tzu's *The Art of War*, or what is more accurately translated into as the single word of "Strategy." Sun Tzu was a practical philosopher who wrote the 7,000-word *The Art of War* in about 500 B.C.

Many of Sun Tzu's teachings are applied today in nearly every facet of personal and business life. Interesting comparisons for sure, and while I suspect no one believes in every one of his principles, there are a few we can use to be better leaders, decision makers, husbands, wives, friends...and strategists.

Attached is our agenda for Bing-Fa. Be ready to present your area in any way you find necessary. Use any medium you prefer, including slides, handouts, pure discussion, or debate. Please present your groups' issues and opportunities, and then some of the thoughts and plans (and of course budgets) you feel are needed to get there.

There will be those that concur and those that disagree. The idea is to get all ideas out and then set a course for both strategy and tactics. One without the other would be a mistake.

Looking forward to this meeting.

Thanks

Dean

We held our first Bing Fa meeting on Catalina Island, owned by the Wrigley family, also owners of the Chicago Cubs. They had originally bought the island for spring training purposes, tired of their team being spied on in Florida. They built a baseball field and a mansion on top of the hill, and from the master bedroom William Wrigley used binoculars to watch his team train. I felt his secrecy was kind of in line with what Sun Tzu talked about.

Our first Bing Fa meeting, Catalina Island, 2004.

We held our meetings at the mansion. I gave everyone readings from *The Art of War* and each day we started off by discussing a passage and how it applied to our challenges at Alteryx. I helped the team think through these ideas without me imposing my thoughts on them. We were all discovering its relevance and potential applications together.

At the end of the two-and-a-half-day meeting, we made the most significant decision we ever made as a company—to take all of our individual products and weave them into a single platform. The decision to build Alteryx was universally agreed to. We were off and running.

I've used Bing Fa as the theme for all our company-wide get-togethers ever since; for the last 17 years, we've had two such face-to-face meetings annually. And we almost always have had weekly, quarterly, and monthly calls with Bing Fa stakeholders. Up until my retirement, the core issue we continued to discuss was the alignment of strategy and tactics.

Bing Fa was known for not constraining anyone. I didn't seek agreement or consensus prior to our meetings. I went in with an open mind, wanting to hear everyone's ideas, without assumptions or preconceptions.

In the early days we had spirited, even highly contentious discussions. A couple of times it almost came to fisticuffs, especially in the early going when we were still trying to figure out the product/ market fit and everyone was opinionated and certain they had the right idea. But fortunately we never had to call the cops or rush anyone to the hospital.

We always went to an off-site venue, a lodge or a nice hotel, to make sure the team wasn't distracted. As the stakes got bigger and bigger, we rented a house in Hawaii and I brought in a private chef because I didn't want the team to waste time leaving the house for meals. We stayed together and became highly focused for three or four days. We ate, slept, and dreamt what we were trying to accomplish, an organization of fledgling leaders that had never before encountered these challenges.

In 2007, three years into Bing Fa, the big discussion was about the cloud. Everyone was saying the cloud was the future and we weren't in that mode yet, although we knew that our software development cycles would improve if we were cloud-based. It would be easier to create fixes, updates, and enhancements, and require customers to be on the latest version. We could do more testing and experimenting with user interfaces. So many advantages would ensue.

I remember throwing out a potential strategy. Why not take our Alteryx designer product and make it a browser-based application? If nothing else, customers would want it to ease their deployment options, even if it wasn't a cloud-only play.

Boy, was that a heated debate. I don't know if I offended people who couldn't wrap their arms around the idea or if they just thought I was heading down the wrong path. Yet no one presented any really good alternative ideas. We had been experimenting with a cloud-based solution for several years, so it didn't fall on completely deaf ears, but it did force people to think more critically about the big issues.

So Bing Fa has had its difficult moments, whether the focus was the budgeting process, career planning for the hundreds of people we were hiring annually, product strategy, go-to-market actions, acquisition discussions, and everything in between. Bing Fa was 50% tension and 50% harmony, and I loved that mix.

The major point is that we needed to have these frank, even contentious moments, and a framework for discussing them. Think of a marriage or friendship or family relationship where problems are encountered, not discussed, and swept under the rug. Most of us know how that turns out. You need a framework for addressing conflicts, for bringing them out in the open where they can be recognized and resolved. It may not be Bing Fa for you, but you need some kind of specific framework to make this happen.

Sun Tzu said that if your enemy is easily provoked, then pick on him because you want to take people out of their game. One instance in which we provoked competitors was related to Clayton Christensen's idea of disruptive innovation.

We were going down that path by disrupting the practice of data science, which used to be accessible only to 2 million trained statisticians in the world, the people with "Ph.D." after their names. We knew that if we could pull off what J.C.R. Licklider was saying— reducing the friction between humans and computers in a complex area like data science—we could disrupt an old discipline and make it many times larger.

Around 2008 Google rolled out Google Maps, and specifically the Google Maps API (or Application Programming Interface, a software intermediary that allows two applications to talk to each other. Each time you use an app like Facebook, send an instant message, or check the weather on your phone, you're using an API. To simplify, an API delivers a user response to a system and sends the system's response back to a user). By doing so, Google disrupted the multi-billion-dollar GIS (geographic information systems) industry.

We didn't want to be left out of their excitement because we had the ability to ride their coattails.

We had a little-known API of our own to perform demographic research. We integrated it with the Google Maps API, and we ran a press release about it titled "Business Intelligence with Google." We got Google very upset, as evidenced by the cease-and-desist letter from their legal department. While our API was powerful, it paled in comparison to what Google had released. Yet, when you're weak, act strong, and we sort of outdid what Google had by latching onto their accomplishment.

They didn't sue us. They told us we couldn't run press releases like that without their approval. I didn't really care. Sun Tzu would have approved.

Another example of creative provocation is when we ran a guerilla marketing campaign against the SAS Institute, a software company co-founded and led by James Goodnight since 1976. They've been at $3 billion in revenue for many years because their market capped out and they couldn't disrupt themselves to grow larger. Anyone who could use SAS was already using SAS.

They didn't understand that Clayton Christensen was right, that if someone else came along and made their hard software easy to use, they would get punished in the process. We had added an open-source technology in our software called Open Source R, the old programming language for data science and the precursor to Python. We made it really easy for people to build statistical models in our software. I didn't want to spend a lot of money on it because we were still light in VC funding, having just received our Series A money.

So how did we get some attention without spending any money?

We ran a campaign against the SAS Institute, a little over the top but fun as hell. We had three three-minute videos on YouTube that poked fun at their technology for being old, hard to use, and expensive, available to only the few. We poked them right in the eye in a hilarious way and we got a million views on these videos. Another cease-and-desist letter but well worth it.

If people are only thinking tactically in a business, then everyone's going in scattered directions. Everyone's got a great idea. There's often no shortage of them. But making ideas into reality is kind of tough.

In the early days of Alteryx and at various stages in the company's growth, most people on my team knew tactically what to do. I don't think they always knew *why* they were doing it. My team would chuckle every time I reminded them: "If you don't know where you're going, any road will get you there."

As a result, we ended up wasting a bunch of time and effort. Five years ago one of my teams spent probably five or six man-years and a couple of million dollars building a software product without knowing what the objective was. They thought their tactics were spot-on, yet they didn't achieve the stated objective of getting to the cloud. Most companies fail on establishing good, sound strategy that everyone can agree on; instead, they waste time and money doing a bunch of work for work's sake.

Despite Bing Fa, I wasn't sufficiently aligning strategic objectives with tactical execution. I had to grow into this myself in terms of mastering that balance.

I knew strategically what was necessary. What I wasn't good at was articulating that strategy. Sometimes you're so close to an idea or a problem that you become blinded. What I thought was obvious to me wasn't obvious to others. I probably didn't do a good enough job at selling some of the strategic vision.

And the people who did understand the vision didn't know how to communicate it to their teams. If you asked the employees why they were doing something a certain way, they'd probably say, "I was told to do this" or "I'm doing this because that's the way we've always done it." You're on a treadmill where you get burned out on the tactics and lose sight of the big picture. *What is the big picture? What are we trying to do? What impact are we having?* The workforce needs to be reoriented to that big picture. And it has to be repeated often and with great consistency.

In 2015 I put a lot of thought into figuring out how to get people pointed in the right direction. We've always had company 'town hall' meetings and "ask me anything" forums, but now we had global kickoffs and quarterly all-hands meetings focused on strategy.

I learned as a leader that you have to repeat most things 10 times before anyone gets it. Maybe more than 10 times, just like with kids—you tell them 10 times not to touch the stove and they still manage to get burned.

At our annual Bing Fa event we'd spend three days collaborating on the right strategic direction and what needed to be done by functional areas. And then we'd go back to work and by the end of the next quarter none of the stuff we discussed had gotten done. People forgot what the strategy was. Extremely frustrating.

While I always had company-wide imperatives and a mission statement, those kinds of frameworks have always troubled me, only because they're esoteric and broad enough to help people understand the mission of the company, the vision, and the overall goal. But every year there has to be some compelling goal that drives you to achieve the big stuff.

So I started creating strategic objectives, calling them "imperatives" to create a sense of urgency and responsibility. These were the things we *had* to do to be successful. Not what we aspired to or would like to do, not the whims of the day or dreams about what Alteryx might become in the future, but the imperatives of the present moment that *had* to happen to maintain our success.

Every year I would create no more than five strategic imperatives.

As mentioned before, my team wasn't good at repeating what I was saying to their teams. Not only did I have to repeat myself 10 times for my leaders to get it, but I lacked storytellers—people who could take my words and translate them clearly and compellingly for their teams in every weekly town hall or staff meeting. Successful businesses have lots of storytellers because the CEO cannot scale the company alone.

To be more focused and proactive in understanding imperatives and aligning everyone's tactics to those imperatives, we created something called "Plan on a Page," where every employee had to go through the imperatives at the beginning of the year. I would roll it out in November to give associates and their leaders time to prepare their plans. They were "big picture" enough so that everyone knew what their functional team had to commit to tactically to achieve them.

I wouldn't let people into our global annual kickoff unless they brought their Plans on a Page with them. It was their passport, evidence that they had a map to translate strategy into tactics.

It got better over time, but again, it's probably the hardest thing to do. In the end, for some people, it's just a job. They want to be busy all day and be told what to do, as opposed to being creative in reaching objectives in the most efficient and effective ways.

One of the most valuable things a software company can have is product telemetry. That means we have visibility inside our software into every button that people push. We know definitively how the customer uses the product. These aren't blind tests or surveys. This is definitive—I know exactly how Mary uses our product every day. I know when she logs on, I know what buttons she pushes and in what order, and I know how long the process takes. When you have a software product, this is perfect knowledge. You know what works and what doesn't work for your customers.

We know a lot about our customers—what industry they're in, what their titles are, and how long they've been using our products. So we had the longitudinal data to make telemetry possible, yet we struggled with it for the longest time.

It wasn't a question of complexity. Rather, it was not understanding the importance of telemetry. If you're an engineer building software, you would think you would want to know how people use the thing you built, but getting people to think that way is hard. And so we started demanding that every time you build something, you must have the ability to track telemetry. Even after doing this for a few years, we still had engineers who didn't understand. In most cases, they weren't told by their leaders of its importance.

I finally made telemetry an imperative. If you're in product marketing or product management at Alteryx, you can't build the next button unless you know how people use all the existing buttons. You should know how people use the product in order to know how to market it to a range of customers. Especially from a company as customer-centric as Alteryx.

Even though we finally figured it out, it's still somewhat of a struggle because people don't always want to believe that it's ground truth for how people use your product.

For a long time, perfecting "Trial to Win" and telemetry remained two of our most nagging issues.

It seems obvious that it's important to think strategically first, agree on a forward strategy, and then define tactically what you need to do to achieve the strategy. But maybe that's not always the case.

There are three components to any successful venture: the *what*, the *why*, and the *how*. Unfortunately, a lot of people start with the how when you first have to know what it is you're trying to accomplish and why you're trying to do it. Only then can you figure out the how.

But when you're a startup, sometimes your craft is the how, not the why or the what.

My lead independent board member is Chuck Corey, who joined us in 2016. He was the chairman of tech investment banking at Morgan Stanley for more than 33 years and probably took more companies public, including Google, than any human on the planet.

He told me how he met Larry Page and Sergey Brin when they were working in their garage. Just a great story. They were thinking about raising money and maybe going public.

Chuck asked them, "What is it that you have?

"We have these cool algorithms."

"Well, how are you gonna make money with that?"

They didn't know. Chuck told them, "You're going to have a hard time going public with that as your pitch."

Look how that turned out.

You could say the same about Bill Gates and Steve Jobs. They were enamored with doing one thing well, not knowing exactly how it would turn out.

Jobs apparently got beat up a lot by the tech analyst community when he first came out with the Mac because it didn't really do anything. MacPaint and MacWrite were the only things it had and the research community said, "Are you crazy? This is not gonna go over very well." They weren't sure what his vision was, other than democratizing computing. Jobs didn't know exactly how to do it, so he made something where you could type in some words and paint some pictures.

Jobs' response to the analyst community was memorable.

"Listen, in every airplane there is a first-class and a coach section, but both sections land at the same time. So you better at least be on the plane, you can figure out how to get into first class later on."

So there are entrepreneurs who benefited from perfect timing. They knew the how, but the why and the what weren't completely figured out. They figured it out later.

But those are the exceptions, not the rule.

The Art of War reminded me of our family dinner table discussions, where we had a lot of give and take and debate. What if we chose a college and didn't like it? What if we chose a profession we would later regret?

Our conversations were far-ranging.

As the youngest, I was more of an observer than a participant and listened closely. My mother would remind me that God gave me one mouth and two ears so I should use them proportionally. I remember my siblings talking about the need to practice in sports, about the need to study if you wanted to get good grades and go to a good college. It was about applying oneself with discipline. It was a family lesson in composing.

Long before *The Art of War*, I was exposed to the relationship between strategy and tactics. My brother Robin could have gone to almost any college in the world. As a high school junior, he had offers from the ten top gymnastics schools in the country. The question for him wasn't what school to go to, but rather what career to pursue, knowing there wouldn't be too many job offers for a gymnast after graduation.

Dad was more focused on Robin's interest in sports because the scholarship offers relieved some of his anxiety about paying tuition for five kids. Mom was more concerned about what he was going to do after college. What happened if he didn't make the Olympics? Then what? She was already looking far ahead, just as she had when dad took the big leap to start his business.

Those conversations weren't a hell of a lot different from Bing Fa. It was more contentious at Bing Fa because we weren't related. No fists were thrown, but there was harsh language and name-calling for sure.

But that was okay. I wanted to allow for a process where people felt they could vent a little bit, speak their minds, and justify a particular strategic direction that they thought we should go with. I've long told my teams that "you have to sell with facts and in the absence of facts you must sell with passion." I wanted honest feedback, although sometimes it was hard to hear. Without feedback, we have a hard time seeing other points of view and seeing ourselves. We can take ourselves too seriously and become myopic in vision.

Every process and relationship should have a feedback loop where we can give and receive honest and constructive criticism.

Most of the big strategic decisions we made at Alteryx came from the give and take of Bing Fa. Sun Tzu saw clearly into how to use your resources wisely and conservatively.

Out of all my mentors, he gave me the most confidence. And nothing gets me more excited than meeting people in Silicon Valley who are also fans of *The Art of War*.

Chapter Ten

Influencers and Inspirations

Being a CEO is lonely. There weren't a lot of people I could talk to, especially during the first 14 years when I had no investors. Normally you would call your investor to seek some advice or to have a shoulder to cry on. They gave you a bunch of money, they believed in you, and you could tell them what was going on in the company, your opportunities and your challenges, and get some good, honest feedback. But I didn't have that option and it was tough.

So I relied on the thinkers I had long admired, and new ones I discovered along the way.

I had heard Buckminster Fuller talk many years before starting the business, at a conference on world affairs. I was in college at the time and only went because dad loved the guy and urged me to go with him. He admired his philanthropic thinking and his urgency around saving the world from all of its problems, but what dad admired most of all was that Fuller was a great thinker—a design engineer, an architect, a systems theorist.

Fuller talked for a very long time—about architecture and design and war and exploring space. It was all over the place but so intriguing.

But then he stopped, and the worried look on his face caught my attention. "The truth is," he said, "we're building all the right technologies for all the wrong reasons." He took a deep breath and continued. "We're never going to be able to take care of Spaceship Earth very well nor for very long if we don't see it as a common cause. It has to be all of us."

That statement has stuck with me for years and years. Especially as our company has matured, and our focus shifted from inward to outward thinking, to our evolved role in the world. But I don't think I fully realized the impact he had on me until we started Alteryx for Good in 2016. It was Fuller's sense that we all have a larger responsibility to the environment and society, that our vision needs to be larger than the bottom line, which inspired our philanthropy.

We don't gift the world to our kids. They inherit it from us. And our obligation is to make sure that they're inheriting something that's better than what we got. That challenge is more pressing and more daunting than ever before. Buckminster Fuller tied it to my craft— using technology for the right ends.

I didn't know this at the time because I didn't plan at 19 to start a software company. But it eventually caught up with me and now it's probably the most common story I tell at every new associate bootcamp and in almost every press interview I've ever given.

People have always asked me, "Who were your mentors?" Other than my father, the first name I mention is Buckminster Fuller.

Another is J.C.R. Licklider. I don't come across many tech executives who know who he is, but I tell everybody that if there's anything they should read, it's Licklider's *Man-Computer Symbiosis*, the seminal paper he published in 1960.

He's credited largely with having been the primary influence in the creation of online banking, the computer mouse, and the graphical user interface. He knew that if you could remove the friction between humans and the computer, everybody wins. You combine the linear, computational capabilities of the machine with human logic to create a true symbiotic relationship.

While he's unknown to most contemporary tech execs, all the great founders in the Valley know who Licklider was because he encouraged and motivated them to build better products.

Rather than engage in a debate about whether artificial intelligence was more important than human intelligence, or whether the Singularity would come to pass (super-intelligent machines that surpass human cognitive ability), Licklider believed the Singularity would never come to pass if we took away the friction between the human and the computer. That's because we'll always have a human who's more responsive to the machine, and we'll always have a machine that's more responsive to a human. The strengths of *both* will increase.

In *Man-Computer Symbiosis*, Licklider talks about the most perfect symbiotic relationship on planet earth—that between the fig tree and the fig wasp.

> The fig tree is pollinated only by the insect *Blastophaga grossorun*. The larva of the insect lives in the ovary of the fig tree, and there it gets its food. The tree and the insect are thus heavily interdependent: the tree cannot reproduce without the insect; the insect cannot eat without the tree; together, they constitute not only a viable but a productive and thriving partnership. This cooperative "living together in intimate association, or even close union, of two dissimilar organisms" is called symbiosis.
>
> Man-computer symbiosis is a subclass of man-machine systems. There are many man-machine systems. At present, however, there are no man-computer symbioses.

The fig wasp inseminates the tree, the tree grows fruit, and the wasp eats the fruit.

The tree and the wasp can't live without each other. They bring out the best in each other. The same can be true, Licklider noted, for the human brain and the computing machine.

> The hope is that, in not too many years, human brains and computing machines will be coupled together very tightly, and that the resulting partnership will think as no human brain has ever thought and process data in a way not approached by the information-handling machines we know today.

I didn't truly understand the fig tree/fig wasp comparison until I was travelling in Argentina. I saw huge trees with big trunks and droopy branches, and there were the big wasps eating the fruit. Everything kind of clicked. *Oh my God, that's it.*

I wouldn't say we designed Alteryx or our software around that concept, but at the end of the day we kind of knew that you had to make the hard simple, and the way you do that is exactly what Licklider was talking about—you've got to take away the friction.

If you can do that with fewer keystrokes, with user interfaces and experiences that are fun and engaging, the hard becomes simple. I used to joke that if I had to rename the company, I'd call it Fig Tree Software.

There are a whole bunch of people who predicted that the Singularity would be here by 2020. Now they're pushing it out to 2040.

Like Licklider, I've never believed that the Singularity will occur. Not in 2040, not in 2080, not ever. And that's because if we're building the right software, we're going to amplify human intelligence.

Alan Turing, the renowned mathematician and computer scientist, played a pivotal role in cracking Germany's Enigma machine during World War II and is widely considered the father of artificial intelligence. Yet, only when he inserted human logic into his code-breaking process was he able to crack Enigma. The Germans sent out a newly encoded message every day but there was a repetition in the messages that required human logic to solve. The machine didn't have that logic.

Turing was also the first to test machine learning against a human counterpart with the aptly named "Turing Test" of 1950. It was designed to see if a machine could exhibit behavior that was indistinguishable from that of a human. While there are now many kinds of artificial intelligence that can pass the Turing Test, the most advanced mission-critical scenarios, such as autonomous vehicles or military drones, require human input.

Turing proved that the Singularity wouldn't take place. Like

Licklider, he believed that in its place you'll have amplified human intelligence. That doesn't mean there won't be artificial intelligence, but I personally don't think we're going to rely on machines exclusively.

When we think about the future of our world, it's easy to focus on the shiny objects and technology that make our lives easier: flying cars, 3D printers, digital currencies, and automated everything. Advancements in AI and technology are meant to make our lives easier, yet they pose a threat to society when they are not perfect.

We face many challenges with AI, from tech and social media giants controlling speech on their platforms, to services and technologies that speed up processes but apply unintentional bias. When we start relying on algorithms to make decisions for us, that's when things begin to take a turn for the worse. AI can't just be good enough for us to create a better world for ourselves—it must be perfect.

Here's why.

A study from MIT found that gender classification systems sold by several major tech companies had an error rate as much as 34.4 percentage points higher for darker-skinned females than lighter-skinned males. Likely due to skewed data sets, examples like this present a myriad of problems in decision making, especially in employment recruiting and criminal justice systems. Algorithms that exclude female candidates for traditionally male-dominated jobs, or that determine a criminal's "risk score" based on appearance versus actions, are only amplifying the biases that we should be removing.

All humans have blind spots, so the creation of models and algorithms should involve careful human interaction and not just more powerful machines. Otherwise, the use of AI risks becoming irresponsible at best and unethical at worst, even putting our First Amendment rights at risk.

One study from the University of Washington found that leading AI models for identifying hate speech were one-and-a-half times more likely to flag tweets as offensive or hateful when they were written by African-Americans. Biases in hate-speech tools have the potential to unfairly censor speech on social media, allowing expression by only by select groups of people or individuals. By implementing a "human in the loop" approach, people get the final say in decision making and black-box bias can be avoided.

When we start relying on AI to make decisions for us, it often does more harm than good. Last year, *WIRED* published an article called "Artificial Intelligence Makes Bad Medicine Even Worse," which highlights how diagnoses powered by AI aren't always accurate, and when they are, they're not always necessary to treat. Imagine getting screened for cancer without having any symptoms and being told that you do in fact have cancer, but later finding out that it was just something that looks like cancer because the algorithm was wrong.

While advancements in AI should be changing healthcare for the better, AI in an industry like this absolutely must be regulated in a way where the human is making the final decision or diagnosis rather than a machine. If we remove the human from the equation and fail to regulate ethical AI, we risk making detrimental errors in crucial, everyday processes.

Alan Turing gives me cover whenever I get into arguments with people about the Singularity. They'll say, "Can't you see what's happening with microchips and the power of computers? They're going to be able to solve *anything*."

My reply? "Well, with all our technology, were we able to predict or prevent or eradicate COVID?"

It's problematic to think that our inventions are going to somehow replace us or have the answers for everything. Both Turing and Fuller are questioning technology while trying to advance it; they're challenging it in certain ways, by asking more of it, and that fascinates me as the co-founder of a major tech company.

Andre Geim, the Dutch-British physicist and Nobel Prize winner, probably wouldn't have said he was an expert at many things. While he had a day job, he said he learned the most during what he called his "Friday night experiments." Sensible Socks, portable cribs, and chimneyless fireplaces were Friday night experiments for me, where I was dabbling and trying to figure out what moved me and what potential opportunities existed. They were also attempts, although I didn't realize it at the time, to remove friction between people and a product. I was using the insights of Licklider, which would later be applied to how we designed software at Alteryx. I stumbled upon this instinctively, intuitively, through experimentation.

Geim invented graphene, one of the most important elements ever invented, primarily used in computer chips. He discovered it by accident during one of his Friday night experiments when he was messing around with some colleagues.

They had been trying all kinds of things when they poured some water into a bottle and then a little bit of graphite in it and mixed it up. Presto!

Geim's point was that a lot of the most important things that people build in this world weren't necessarily intentional. In fact, one of the drug companies recently said that their vaccine for COVID was developed as a result of a mistake. Geim discovered an extremely important element by grazing shallow.

You can't always plan on building (or disrupting) the next great mousetrap. Sometimes you stumble on it.

Geim's ideas influenced how we built our platform. We've always said to customers that our software can be used to solve almost any problem. You can use our software to engage in Friday night experiments much like Geim or I did. You can do analytics in the financial planning and analysis department, or on the legal team, or in sales and marketing operations. You can do analytics in almost any functional area in almost any industry, grazing shallow until you find your sweet spot, and then you want to go deep.

Did we have that "Geim kind of experience" in the early days of Alteryx, where we had to stumble around and graze shallow?

After Integration Technologies, I knew where the core competencies had to be around spatial analytics. I didn't really know the extent of what we were trying to build and the market for it. A lot of entrepreneurs go all-in and end up regretting what they built because they didn't really understand who they were selling to. They didn't know how people were going to utilize a piece of software. And in the early days I certainly didn't know the complete range of use cases that our platform could address until we talked to customers who were conducting Friday night experiments with it.

We had done a real estate deal with Walmart to help them build out their store network. In one of our meetings they made a presentation about all the things they loved about our platform, the first time a customer had ever done that. And in the last slide of the presentation, they also made some recommendations for what they would like to see changed.

"We're the finance team, and you guys don't have any financial formula libraries in your platform."

I had gone so deep into geospatial that I hadn't thought about other use cases. On the way back to the airport I called Ned.

"I think we overlooked something that's now patently obvious."

"What's that?"

"We have no financial formulas and the world's largest retailer is now demanding them."

I could almost hear him smack his forehead. "Oh my gosh, I can't believe we missed that."

And so grazing shallow is really valuable until you find the sweet spot for your product, career, business, or almost anything else you do in life. And then you go deep. Thirty days later we had financial formulas built into our formula editor.

My mentors made me a better thinker, leader, and person, and, other than my father, I never met a single one of them.

CHAPTER ELEVEN

Yes, You Can Change the World

In Act Two of your journey you've passed through a few swamps and have become better at composing. The path is easier. People get you because you've gotten to know who you are, and that has led to your success. But once you've become successful in whatever your journey is, you realize there's something more to it than that.

Fuller spoke about our compulsion to develop technology for all the wrong reasons. He worried about the world that our children are inheriting, about our larger responsibility to the environment and society. Like Turing, he knew technology's limits.

Has their thinking influenced how we run Alteryx? Am I concerned about whether our technology is being used in negative ways? Do I want to orient the company in a way where the technology would be used to fight climate change or battle COVID rather than— to use an extreme example—build a better bomb or improve battlefield scenarios?

Most entrepreneurs, when they're struggling in their early days to slow their burn rate of cash or worrying about how they're going to make payroll, aren't concerned about being "good deed doers" and giving their software away free to non-profits and universities.

Fuller invented the first autonomous vehicle and his big claim to fame was the geodesic dome, which must have provided him with some royalties, but I don't think he made much money. I don't know if he died penniless, but he invented lots of things without much financial reward and maybe that was because he put too much emphasis on doing good.

Someone's got to pay for doing good because building software doesn't come cheap. As an entrepreneur, the last thing I wanted to do was give everything away pro bono.

There was an inflection point in 2016 where we wanted to give back more.

A lot of young Millennials were coming into the workforce looking for a north star. They wanted more than a good job that paid well and where they could build cool things. They wanted to give back to society in meaningful ways.

Once Alteryx became established, the warnings of Buckminster Fuller became more present and urgent in my thinking.

Are there people who use our software to do nefarious things? Probably. Just like someone can legally buy a gun and do something stupid with it.

I try not to worry too much about the bad stuff. I'm more worried that people aren't going to use our technology to address enough of the important stuff. Like Fuller said, we're never going to be able to take care of Spaceship Earth very well or for very long until we see saving the Earth as a common cause. I heard that in college and have never forgotten it.

In 2016 we launched our Alteryx for Good program, designed to deliver the game-changing benefits of breakthrough data science and analytics capabilities to nonprofit organizations and universities around the world. The thinking behind it was this: if Walmart can use our software to pick the right locations, banks to do derivatives modeling, and airlines to hedge fuel, how come we can't use it to solve pressing, everyday problems? Like bringing dignity back to the homeless? Or solving the opioid crisis? Eradicating malaria or protecting endangered species? Or making it easier for hospitals to function during a global pandemic?

We write a lot of checks for noble causes but simply writing a check is certainly not fulfilling. Just like letting someone else build something that you could build yourself isn't very fulfilling. When you write a check, it feels like skimming to a certain extent. You're doing the easy work while letting others do the harder, more fulfilling work.

I found out that giving money away is much harder than making it. It's very difficult to know where it's going to be best used to address problems effectively and not go to a lot of fluff or overhead. It's another complicated journey. You have to figure out what you're trying to accomplish, and where and how to do that. A Bing Fa for giving would be a good starting point!

Much of our philanthropic work at Alteryx and my personal philanthropy centers on education. In my view, education in this country is utterly broken. I didn't attend my college graduation from UC Boulder because I was anxious to get started on my career. Why celebrate something that had yet to yield anything? As it turned out, other than my organizational behavior class and my Semester at Sea experience, those four years and the countless credits earned were hardly useful in my work. And when I got my M.B.A. degree at Pepperdine, where I learned little of business value, I truly knew that higher learning was broken.

My wife Angie and I moan about the state of education all the time. So much of what we learn in school isn't practical in our lives. There should be required courses in high school about navigating relationships and parenting, and building one's emotional intelligence. That's far more important than calculus. I would have used parenting classes far more than I've used algebra or chemistry.

For many roles in life, we require proper training. You can't drive a car without passing a test. You need a license to cut someone's hair. But for two of the most difficult tasks in life, if not the most difficult— marriage and child-rearing—we require no training at all. And we wonder why the divorce rates are sky high.

And when a marriage ends, it becomes a punitive system when the lawyers take over. Yet there's nothing that's done proactively on the other side, to teach young people about relationships and emotional intelligence. The lawyers probably have a lobby in Washington saying we don't need any parenting or marriage classes for young people.

A large part of the problem with education is that people get put on a journey before they've discovered their path. Young kids are coming out of high school with little exposure to the world around them, and suddenly they're being asked to declare a major. Your mother was a judge, so you decide to follow in her path. Your father was a nurse, so you choose that direction.

Many of them, if not most, have no idea whether that choice is the right one. Does the major match your strengths, passion, personality, and expectations? Or are you simply following the safe route that your parents want you to take? Picking your major at the age of 20 is useless in my opinion because you risk being miserable by following someone else's passion.

I've talked to so many people who came out with an English degree and who are now working in computer science, or who majored in data science and are now musicians.

I've always been turned off by the fact that academia gives you a deadline to make a commitment to go in a certain direction. And on top of that, you come out with a collective trillion and a half dollars of student debt. You hate your career, you're up to your neck in loan payments, and it isn't pretty. Fixing education must be a priority.

I didn't choose my major until the last possible moment because I didn't want to waste my money. Before I went on the trip around the world, I fortunately picked international business as my major because I was so intrigued by traveling and it was the only major that excited me. I didn't want to go into finance or marketing because it wasn't me; they seemed like majors with limitations.

Back in the 1980s, if you didn't have a Master's degree your career would be hampered. It was kind of an expectation that you worked for one year and then got one. So, I went to Pepperdine at night for nine months while I played Mr. Mom during the day, taking care of Reed, our newborn, while my wife went back to work. I learned more in those nine months about life, love, ambitions, and dreams than any education could ever provide. I came out with an

M.B.A. from a good university, but I didn't really learn a whole lot, and certainly nothing that I've put into practice today. (And then there's Bill Gates, Steve Jobs, and Mark Zuckerberg, none of whom graduated with degrees, and you realize success isn't based on traditional education.)

So I don't think academia in its traditional forms is necessary. Maybe for undergraduates as a social experience, and I certainly don't want my heart surgeon to have a Nano degree off the Udacity network.

But there are two lessons here:

1. No one can pick your journey; you have to discover or stumble on it yourself.
2. Learning isn't a two-, four-, or six-year process—it's lifelong. Always be learning.

If you have the wherewithal to be introspective and understand what your weaknesses are, every part of your journey should help you identify what you don't know. *I know nothing about this subject in front of me, so I better go learn about it.*

If I could do it over again, I would have gone on my world-wide trip and then engaged in six-month Nano degrees twice every year, to learn the skills I didn't yet possess. With the internet today, there's so much opportunity to do that at just a few hundred dollars per class.

Universities in general are way overpriced. They should focus much more on job skills by offering entrepreneurship programs that allow students to become interns right away and shadow executives. You don't know if you want to go into HR until you shadow an HR executive for six weeks. You might realize it's a tough job only suitable for people with thick skin.

At Alteryx we offer an internship program where college kids come in and shadow people, listen in on phone conversations, watch what we do, and both attend and participate in meetings. This helps inform what journey they should be on. They may still not get it right, but at least they're eliminating all the stuff that they know isn't right because mom or grandpa picked it.

There has been a lot of talk about forgiving student debt. I think that sends the wrong message. Instead, we should be retrofitting academia. We should put caps on how much they can charge. As Geim would say, let these kids graze shallow, let them experiment. And don't bankrupt them in the process.

Here's an example. We have an employee whose son planned to attend the University of British Columbia to study data analytics, maybe computer programming. His father had encouraged him to go down that path, yet he wasn't completely sure that was the path he wanted.

We hired him as an intern before he started at the university and he shadowed me. I brought him to meetings and had him present to CEOs of global companies—yes, at the age of 18. It was eye-opening. You could see that he learned more in six weeks by shadowing a few of my executives than he did in his entire high school career. It was much more rewarding for him than choosing the path that had the richest reward or the biggest title.

Colleges should focus on that kind of job training, so young people get a sense of what they like and don't like, what they're good at or not so good at. At a minimum, it allows them to eliminate journeys that they're positively not interested in and to get on the right journey sooner.

How did all this affect the way we view and run our philanthropy program Alteryx for Good?

College is hard enough for kids whose parents have the money to pay for it or the ability to get a loan, but what about all the kids who don't have that opportunity? They're starting their lives with few prospects. *Their journey is drugs, gangs, welfare, and homelessness.*

If we really believe that learning is lifelong and we don't want kids to take out big loans (I know people who've been out of school for two decades and they're still paying off their college loans), then we radically have to change education in this country.

We offer the SparkED program to empower learners of all skill levels, across every field of study, to develop their data analytics abilities. The program is run by Libby, one of my co-founders, who has also found her sweet spot. Educators and learners receive free access to Alteryx software, learning materials, certifications, and a vibrant online community. They can easily perform data preparation, blending, reporting, modeling, and much more in a no-code/low-code, drag-and-drop interface. We have learners from over 600 educational institutions in 39 countries, and our resources are available in English, French, German, Japanese, Portuguese, Spanish, and Chinese.

Our focus is to offer young people Nano degrees online, at low cost. We offer generous scholarship assistance and a range of courses. If someone takes a six-month course in Python coding only to discover it's not to their taste, that's a win. They can pick something else that intrigues them and we'll pay for another scholarship.

In addition to our emphasis on education, we offer software assistance to individuals and non-profits to address a wide range of social and environmental issues. I couldn't have been more excited to be part of our efforts during the COVID pandemic. Our software helped hospitals predict when they were going to run out of beds and how to distribute protective equipment. We helped hospitals in New York reimagine their supply chains. And we were providing additional COVID-related assistance to many countries around the world.

When COVID hit one of my sales engineers, Peter Abrahmson, came to me and said, "Dean, we're helping lots of people, but what are we going to do about the 30 million people who are out of work?"

We started a program called ADAPT (Advancing Data and Analytics Potential Together). We put this together in less than 30 days back in April 2020, a month after COVID hit. We supplied anyone who was unemployed or furloughed with a free piece of Alteryx software that normally sells for $4,000 per year. We put them into our learning programs, where they could become certified in Alteryx and earn a Nano degree in business analytics in just four weeks. We educated around 12,000 people in a very short period of time.

Much more rewarding than writing a check.

In addition to giving away $300 million of free software, we work with a little more than 500 nonprofit organizations around the world. Whether they're bringing dignity back to the homeless in San Francisco, or eradicating malaria in Zambia, or fighting forest fires in Australia, our software is there to help. There has been nothing on my journey more rewarding than this.

This is especially important to Millennials today. It's what Generation Z cares about. They don't care about the paycheck as much as working for a socially responsible organization they can believe in. That's a trend and it's a very good one. And yes, part of the impetus behind our philanthropy is to attract talent, but that's not the main reason. I wanted to do it because it's the right thing to do. I think philanthropy largely should be confidential. When you use it as a PR stunt, it probably backfires. On the other hand, it could have a multiplier effect when it's visible.

My wife Angie and I have our own foundation called i-Rise. Our plan is to give away most of our money to help young people earn Nano degrees in areas that excite students. We're dedicated to helping young people find their paths, with as much freedom as we can offer and little or no debt.

In recent years the importance of philanthropy and diversity has become more and more recognized in the investor community. There are Exchange Traded Funds (ETFs), for example, that now invest primarily based upon ESG scores (a numerical measure of how a company is perceived to be performing on a wide range of environmental, social, and governance issues). The thinking is that inclusion, diversity, and philanthropy, done in the right ways, make for better financial outcomes for investors.

And I tend to agree. If you do believe that our differences are our strengths, you would expect that to be true. I think Marc Benioff, CEO of Salesforce, probably started the craze 20 years ago when he developed the 1-1-1 philanthropy model, where he encourages his customers and his partners to give 1% of their profits, 1% of their time, and 1% of their sales to a nonprofit.

But I didn't want to follow someone else's journey; I wanted my own.

Through our Alteryx for Good program, more than 500 nonprofits around the world use our software to optimize fundraising programs, allocate budgets more efficiently, communicate results to major donors and grantors more effectively, and better leverage, engage, and retain volunteers. By collaborating with our Alteryx for Good Co-Lab volunteers, they can make smarter decisions faster, and do it all without burning hours on spreadsheets. Alteryx for Good Co-Lab volunteers help organizations prep data for reporting efficiencies, provide insights about specific tools and functions to train staff or students, or complete an analytic lifecycle to further an organization's initiatives.

In order to solve global warming or reduce carbon emissions or ease the opioid crisis, you need people who have domain and subject matter expertise. A lot of the non-profits didn't have an analyst on staff, so using our software would have been pretty complex to say the least. We therefore allow our employees to donate 1% of their time to any nonprofit, to train them in using the Alteryx platform.

Our volunteer program also provides 20 hours of paid time off for associates to help out in causes of their choice. They are engaged in making a difference in a variety of activities—sorting at donation centers, providing expertise on data-driven projects, planting trees, and many other projects.

A lot of Baby Boomer executives may think: *Why aren't they working instead? Isn't there something better they can do with that time?* Thankfully, that attitude has changed greatly among the younger generation of leaders.

One group we've assisted is LavaMae, in San Francisco. To alleviate the homelessness crisis, they've converted old city buses, installing in them showers, a barber shop, and a small medical clinic. They then drive to various places in San Francisco, park for a day, and homeless people are able to get a shave and a haircut, take a shower, and have their teeth checked. LavaMae used our software to maintain a longitudinal database on their "guests" and to track the care they received over time and other improvements in their lives, such as obtaining employment.

We assisted PATH, a Seattle-based global non-profit dedicated to improving public health. We donated software and volunteers from our staff. They use our platform to address problems with malaria in Zambia. We also assisted a group called the Royal Flying Doctors in Australia, who fly around the country to provide medical assistance to individuals living in remote places too far from care. They use our software to prioritize what parts of the country to visit. They saved enough money from using our platform to purchase another airplane.

We've also collaborated with three data scientists, based in Romania, Canada, and Singapore, who were trying to build a contact tracer for COVID. We helped them develop an app for contact tracing in just a few weeks.

We've also worked with NoSchoolViolence, an organization that tries to identify kids who may be predisposed to violence through early warning signs. They're using our software to analyze a range of data that can point to kids who could be at risk of gun violence, so they can receive support and services.

Our software is bipartisan, used by both the Republican and Democrat parties to harvest voter registration data across the country. They aggregate that data with other information (age, income, marital status, credit scores, digital footprints, etc.) to do micro-targeting to voters.

I would love to take this data and put it into an Alteryx application that would enable the political parties to determine where they have to focus their efforts to convince voters on various issues, whether it's healthcare, gun control, or environmental issues. I would sell this info to the parties, but also have a free website for the public where they could use the data to draw congressional districts that they think are fair and accurate. In effect, we could use data to have a public vote on those districts, instead of suffering through the usual dishonest gerrymandering conducted by both parties.

There is no shortage of ideas for how we can change the world. We just need to have the will and the foresight to bring them alive and make them a reality in our daily lives.

CHAPTER TWELVE

The Little Things Count

I've listened many times to Admiral William McRaven's 2014 commencement speech at the University of Texas at Austin, describing his training to be a Navy SEAL:

> My instructors, who at the time were all Vietnam veterans, would show up in my room, and the first thing they would do is inspect my bed. If I did it right, the corners would be square, the covers would be pulled tight, the pillow centered just under the headboard, and the extra blanket folded neatly at the foot of the rack. This was a simple task, mundane at best, but every morning we were required to make our beds to perfection.
>
> That seemed a little ridiculous at the time, particularly in light of the fact that we were aspiring to be real warriors— tough, battle-hardened Seals. But the wisdom of this simple act has been proven to me many times over.
>
> If you make your bed every morning, you will have accomplished the first task of the day. It will give you a small sense of pride, and it will encourage you to do another task, and another, and another. And by the end of the day, that one task completed will have turned into many tasks completed.
>
> Making your bed will also reinforce the fact that the little things in life matter. If you can't do the little things right, you'll never be able to do the big things right. And if by chance you

have a miserable day, you will come home to a bed that you made, and a made bed gives you encouragement that tomorrow will be better.

So if you want to change the world, start off by making your bed.

I remember my initial reaction to hearing this: *Huh? Make my bed and change the world? Really?* It sounded like glib and simplistic "self-help." Make my bed and stop a pandemic? Make my bed and halt climate change? Make my bed and, over time (23 long years, to be exact), create a multi-billion-dollar company?

Maybe McRaven had a point: if you can't master the discipline to do the simple things, you may never accomplish the big things. The little things are the building blocks for the big things.

That's your task—to do the little things and find out what that one thing is that you do best. Sometimes it's obvious; in most cases it's not. You have to figure out the most important thing to keep your family together, to raise your kids right, to create the masterpiece you've always dreamed of. This is the long emotional journey that only you can start. You have to discover that one thing that you're good at (or need to be good at) in order for your journey to be successful. It took me years to finally find the right product/market fit at Alteryx.

This holds true in many aspects of life. You have to keep the marriage going long enough to find the right fit. Or keep your relationship with your children alive long enough to resolve a difficult past. Or stick with a creative project until you've mastered the discipline or form you've chosen to pursue. Giving up doesn't get you there.

In searching for that one thing you're best at, you will realize you can't build everything yourself. If you try that, you become mediocre at everything and master of nothing.

I learned that lesson early in my career. All the companies I worked for saw data as a valuable asset. But they tried to do it all—they wanted to build the data, the analytics, and the software. I always thought that was a bad idea because from each dollar of investment, 33 cents goes to the team that builds the data, 33 cents goes to the team that builds the analytics, and 33 cents goes to the people who write the software. The investment dollar is not being concentrated on the single thing you do best.

Sure enough, every one of the companies that I worked for and who took that approach ended up being mediocre at everything. They haven't disappeared, but they've been hurt by the competition because they tried to do everything. They didn't trust that other people could help carry the load. They didn't concentrate their resources and people power on their core competency.

Finding your core competency is about knowing your strengths and focusing on them, and realizing that in any relationship, whether it's business or personal, you have to work together as a team and identify what each person's best at.

It's about aligning core competencies with others. In my marriage, Angie's very good at some things and not good at other things. The same goes for me. So I think we're pretty mindful about who should do what. I let her take care of all the detailed stuff because I'm not a super detailed guy. I'm probably a bigger picture guy, more strategic and less tactical.

It's about being self-aware around what you're good at and then bringing it to life. And you can't bring that one thing to life unless you master the little things that skill requires. If you want to change the world but can't make your bed, that's a major disconnect. Without attention to detail and daily discipline in the smallest things—the tactical stuff—your overall strategy cannot be achieved.

I've listened to Admiral McRaven's talk probably hundreds of times. It resonated deeply with me because he described how I had been raised.

My family was very blue-collar, very middle-income. I wasn't given five bucks a week to do chores. I was instructed to make my bed every morning, to put all my clothes away before I went to bed, to clean up after myself in the bathroom after I brushed my teeth. We had one shower for seven of us. So it was incumbent upon all of us to do the right thing, to not be self-centered.

I grew up Catholic. While I don't go to church regularly, my faith is important to me. I pray every night. I do believe that we're here for something more important than just building software or having a strong marriage or raising great kids. We're here to pay it forward and help other people out and do the right thing for others and not just ourselves.

In the dark times, those are the assets that get you through the swamp.

When I heard it from McRaven in a military context, in such a pointed fashion, it clicked with me: *that's what mom and dad were teaching me from a young age.* I learned what discipline was before I knew what the word meant. I learned that the simple, basic things are the foundation for everything else.

One of my favorite quotes is from Steve Jobs: "Life can be much broader once you discover one simple fact: everything around you that you call life was made up by people that were no smarter than you. And *you* can change it—*you* can influence it, *you* can build your *own* things that other people can use... Once you learn that, you'll never be the same again."

That's so powerful because people will give up before they even start a business or begin a journey.

Solving the big things starts with doing the simple things right, one at a time. And each time you accomplish one small thing, you figure out how to accomplish the next harder thing and the next harder thing, and the next harder thing after that.

What's the lyric from the Billie Holiday song?

"The difficult I'll do right now, the impossible will take a little while."

When we started the business, I went in every weekend to vacuum the floor and water the plants, just like dad did in his business. I did it because I didn't have the money to pay someone to do it. But there was another, larger reason: if I wasn't willing to do that kind of stuff, I'd never have the courage to go raise money or hire a bunch of people or open an office in London, followed by 13 other countries.

The discipline of establishing positive habits is so important.

It should be a daily ritual, something taught to your kids at a really early age. They won't recognize what they're being taught, just as I didn't recognize it until years later, but they'll have a solid foundation for the rest of their lives.

I always prayed that my kids would one day tell me they loved me. You only have 18 years to get them ready and then they're on their own. There are no mulligans in child-rearing, no do-overs. So teach them the important life lessons early on—making the bed, caring for family pets, and putting away the groceries.

When my daughter was only seven or eight, she used to follow me around the house, and every time I left a room she would switch off the lights.

I said, "Abby, why are you doing this?"

"I don't want to spend a lot of money on lights."

And I thought, *This is someone who's going to pay attention to the small things.*

These often overlooked disciplines and attitudes are what give you the opportunity to change the world.

When we hire salespeople, I often judge them not necessarily on their background, what they've put on their resume, but at how good they are at selling the resume. Because if you can't sell yourself, you're never going to go anywhere.

The small things are the competency and confidence builders that enable you to sell yourself.

This is crucial if you're going to start your own business. You're in the foxhole all alone, so to speak, and no one else is going to be selling your business for you.

My son Reed has three young sons. I told him, "The most important thing is to show them the value of work. If you don't, they'll never understand why it's important. Simple things—mowing the lawn, painting the house—will help them understand not the value of money, but the value of work."

Whatever project it is, your attitude should be that you're going to do it right. We've lost that in our country, that any kind of work is valuable. We've become enamored of the big achievers, the celebrities, the wealthy and the famous, and the simple trades are looked down on. And that is unfortunate.

McRaven is also talking about the power of hope. Life is not fair and you're going to fail often, but you can't give up. Show up every day, no matter how hard the task before you may appear. Do one small thing right, and then the next. Only then can you complete your journey.

I've reflected often on the small things that have had a profound influence on my career. In 1990, when I was working at Donnelley Marketing Information Services (DMIS), I learned a lesson in doing the small things right by convincing Larry Miller to get out of my office.

That might seem like a strange way to learn a leadership lesson, but only if you've never worked in an office (or with other people in any context, for that matter). It seems like a simple thing, but most of the important lessons in leadership should be simple rather than complex.

When I left my previous job, I was trying to use data more creatively and granularly to achieve better outcomes. At DMIS I was given the role of regional vice president of sales, replacing Larry, who had been there a long time. He was a good sales guy, but he didn't understand many of the servant leadership qualities I've described.

So they gave me his role and on my very first day I walked into his office, which was now my office, and there he was, sitting at what was supposed to be my desk. He didn't want to move out. I thought long and hard about it. Although I instinctually knew what was right, I asked myself a familiar question: *What would dad do?*

I said, "Larry, I don't think it matters what office you're in. You're going to do well regardless of where you sit. But unfortunately you're in my office, at my desk, in my seat, and that doesn't work. By the end of the day, you're going to have to make up your mind."

I knew the entire team I had been hired to lead was watching this unfold. My entire credibility with them would rest on how this turned out.

At the end of the day Larry approached me and said, "Dean, I've thought it over. I'll move down to this office that you're in, and you can go ahead and have my old office."

And we became good friends. I helped him make a ton of money and his career blossomed. He became one of the top reps for the organization. He was happier in his journey and I was happier in mine. It was resolved without drama, with our mutual dignities intact, with no hard feelings.

Had I bungled the office matter—had I pulled rank and ordered him out, and become angry in the process—I would have lost the trust of my team. Had I done nothing and let Larry keep his office, I would have lost their respect. It was a little thing but monumental in its importance. It profoundly influenced my transition into a new position of responsibility.

It wasn't about the size of the office or the fact that it was a corner office. It was about whether and how the two of us could gracefully resolve a conflict without burning bridges. You're never going to be able to change the world if you can't negotiate the hurt feelings of someone you're replacing, while at the same time standing your legitimate ground.

I went home that night with a little jump in my step. I knew that he was on board and I got him to do something that originally he didn't want to do. He went on to crush it. He made a ton of money. He won gigantic accounts and became kind of a folk hero in the company. I was happy for Larry because it wasn't about me. It was about we.

If you want to be successful in whatever journey you're on, it has to be a group effort. It can't be just about your goals and objectives; it has to be about other people's goals and objectives as well.

One day when I was a teenager, my family and I were leaving the church after services. The sermon had been about building legacies and giving back. Philanthropy was not a word I understood way back when.

The priest shook our hands as we walked out of the church and said to my dad, "Bud, when you're dead and gone, and your body is in the casket at the front of this church, and your friends are walking by, what would you like to hear them say?"

IN LOVING MEMORY

1927 - 2012

LAWRENCE REED "BUD" STOECKER

My dad, ages 18 and 84.

The question surprised me. I guess the priest wanted the adults to start thinking about their legacies.

Dad said, "Father, I'd like them to remember me for my great works—that I was a dedicated husband and father." He was too modest to mention that he had volunteered at the church's thrift store every week for years and years.

The priest asked my dad's friend the same question. "Joe, what would you like to hear people say as they pass your open casket?"

"Well, Father, that I gave back to the church, tithed regularly, volunteered at Bingo Night, and was the best provider for my family."

Then it was my mother's turn. I recall looking at her, wondering what she could possibly say that would top those two answers.

"Father," she said, "I'd like to hear them say, 'Look, she's moving.'"

My Mother is an angel because she doesn't get mad, cooks better than a maid and looks good all the time!

Dean Stoecker
1965

1929 - 2008

My winning entry in a local newspaper contest when I was 8 years old.

When we started Alteryx for Good, a lot of it was about giving software away, but there are a lot of things you can do instead of writing checks or making donations. You can go down to the assisted living facility and shake hands with people who have no relatives. You can pack food for the homeless guys on the streets. You can work for racial justice.

I've always said to my associates, "I don't care where you place your time or your money, but you gotta have a passion about giving back to something."

Packing 100,000 meals at our 2019 Global Kick-Off Meeting.

At our global kickoff in 2019, we filled a gigantic ballroom with 1,000 of our employees. Working with an outside agency, we packed over 100,000 meals to meet hunger needs in Southeast Asia. The buzz in the room was electric—laughter, camaraderie, the engaged tumult of a small army hard at work toward a common goal. As I packed boxes side by side with my colleagues, it struck me that we were working together in perfect symbiosis, using the hard-earned wisdom of our individual journeys to address a worthy cause much larger than any one of us.

When we can do that, we can accomplish almost anything.

About the Author

Dean Stoecker was born and raised in Denver, Colorado. He earned his undergraduate degree in International Business from the University of Colorado, Boulder in 1979, and in his senior year became a Shellback, the nautical designation for having sailed around the world during a Semester at Sea, a program then sponsored by the University of Pittsburgh. He earned his MBA from Pepperdine University in Malibu, California.

My Semester at Sea. I'm in the back row, far left.

Dean caught the entrepreneurial bug working with his father and siblings as a teenager, which ultimately led him in 1997 to become the Founder, Chief Executive Officer, and Chairman of the Board of Alteryx, Inc. Twenty years after he started his journey with Alteryx, Dean took the company public on the New York Stock Exchange. Dean retired his CEO role 23 years after founding the company and currently serves as Executive Chairman.

Today, in addition to visiting with the grandkids and walking Truman, their Australian Shepherd, Dean and his wife Angie devote time to their i-Rise Foundation, which seeks to increase opportunities for underserved youth around the world.

For coaching, mentoring, or just a conversation about your journey, feel free to reach out to Dean at dstoecker@alteryx.com.